T0354741

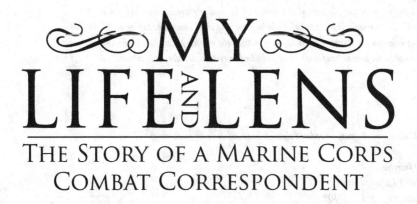

MY LIFE AND LENS

THE STORY OF A MARINE CORPS COMBAT CORRESPONDENT

Captain Robert L. "Bob" Bowen, USMC, Retired

Edited by Robin Kern

MY LIFE AND LENS
THE STORY OF A MARINE CORPS COMBAT CORRESPONDENT

Copyright © 2017 Robert L. Bowen.

All rights reserved. No part of this book may be used or reproduced by any means, graphic, electronic, or mechanical, including photocopying, recording, taping or by any information storage retrieval system without the written permission of the author except in the case of brief quotations embodied in critical articles and reviews.

iUniverse books may be ordered through booksellers or by contacting:

iUniverse
1663 Liberty Drive
Bloomington, IN 47403
www.iuniverse.com
1-800-Authors (1-800-288-4677)

Because of the dynamic nature of the Internet, any web addresses or links contained in this book may have changed since publication and may no longer be valid. The views expressed in this work are solely those of the author and do not necessarily reflect the views of the publisher, and the publisher hereby disclaims any responsibility for them.

ISBN: 978-1-5320-1647-9 (sc)
ISBN: 978-1-5320-2013-1 (hc)
ISBN: 978-1-5320-1646-2 (e)

Library of Congress Control Number: 2017902850

Print information available on the last page.

iUniverse rev. date: 03/17/2017

Cover Photo: Photo made when author was a warrant officer teaching Photojournalism at the Defense Information School in Indianapolis, Indiana, in 1971–1974.

All photos and graphics © by Robert L. Bowen, except where noted.

Chapter 2
Linotype: https://en.m.wikipedia.org/wiki/Linotype_
machine#/media/File%3ALinotype_matrices.png
Composed line with matrices and spacebands: Revised by Paul Koning; Public domain

Chapter 4
Quantico logo: http://www.quanticosentryonline.com/
image_eeffb50a-6b16-11e2-bf17-0019bb30f31a.html

Chapter 6
Okinawa map: https://en.m.wikipedia.org/wiki/Okinawa_
Island#/media/File%3AOkinawa.jpg

Chapter 12
Henderson Hall logo: https://en.wikipedia.org/wiki/
Henderson_Hall_(Arlington,_Virginia)

Chapter 22
Geiger logo: https://en.wikipedia.org/wiki/United_
States_Marine_Corps_School_of_Infantry

Chapter 24
Map of Vietnam: courtesy of Robin Kern

Chapter 26
TBS logo: http://www.usmc-thebasicschool-april1967.com/protect.htm

Chapter 27
Covers of *Ambassadors in Green* and *The Guidebook For Marines*:
Courtesy of Mary Reinwald, Editor, *Leatherneck* Magazine

Chapter 31
Photo of Pentagon: https://en.wikipedia.org/wiki/The_Pentagon#/
media/File:The_Pentagon_US_Department_of_Defense_
building.jpg photo by MSgt Ken Hammond, USAF

Chapter 32
Photo of Skylab: https://en.m.wikipedia.org/wiki/Skylab

Chapter 35
Moving into position to make photo of President Ronald Reagan meeting with
Legionnaires to discuss the POW-MIA issue in the Oval Office on March 16,
1981. (Photo by Jack Kightlinger, courtesy of the Ronald Reagan Library)

In position: (Photo by Jack Kightlinger, courtesy of the Ronald Reagan Library)

The Wall as it appears today with the added "Soldiers"
statue overlooking the black granite wall.
https://i.ytimg.com/vi/I-6F_sxHo1k/maxresdefault.jpg

An aerial view of the National Vietnam Memorial in Washington, D.C. containing
the names of more than 50,000 men and women killed in Vietnam: https://commons.
wikimedia.org/wiki/File:Aerial_view_of_Vietnam_Veterans_Memorial.jpg

Chapter 36
Map of Puerto Rico: https://en.wikipedia.org/wiki/Puerto_Rico

Chapter 37
Official picture of Col Rich Higgins: https://en.wikipedia.org/wiki/William_R._Higgins

Chapter 39
The World Trade Center on 9/11, before the buildings collapsed:
Photo courtesy of Michael Foran, © 2001 Michael Foran.

The Pentagon, where 184 innocent people died on 9/11, plus five Al-Qaeda hijackers.
https://commons.wikimedia.org/wiki/File:Aerial_
photo_of_the_Pentagon,_2001-09-11.jpg

Chapter 40
Legionnaires from around the country gathered in Washington, D.C.,
on several occasions to demonstrate their support for flag protection
legislation: Photo courtesy of *The American Legion* Magazine.

Waiting Game—Legionnaires visit Senator Mitch McConnell's office as the
amendment vote approaches. Much to their chagrin, the senator declined
to meet with them: Photo courtesy of *The American Legion* Magazine.

Da Nang Press Center and the Correspondents Photo Spread
SSgt Steve Stibbens photo. Courtesy of Steve Stibbens. Photo by Horst Faas, AP.

CONTENTS

DEDICATION

This book is dedicated to
My wife, Helen.

My children, Jack, Donna, Bob, Alan, and Brian.

All the men and women I've worked with over the years.

Those who lost their lives with camera, recorder,
or notebook and pen in hand.

Those combat correspondents who survived.

And to my mom who never failed to believe in me
and encourage me to "chase" the story.

FOREWORD

Bob Bowen is one of the most interesting characters who has ever crossed my path in life. I knew him in Vietnam as an aggressive young Marine buck sergeant assigned to *Leatherneck* Magazine.

Bob lived at the difficult intersection of several dominant elements in his life. He had earned his stripes from the ground up in the Marine Corps, but he had the extra imperatives of being assigned to a magazine with a long and proud history. Covering and writing about a war is demanding work, yet sometimes writers can build a story on second-hand accounts from other people or piece together a story in other ways. But there are no shortcuts for a combat photographer: You're in the right place at the right time or you have no picture.

I was in Vietnam as a civilian war correspondent for the Associated Press, and I could make choices about how I covered the stories I was on. Bob had fewer choices. He had editors, but he also had other Marines, many of whom outranked him, who wanted to tell him how to do his job.

True to the "Leatherneck" tradition, he followed the grunts wherever they went.

Like a lot of correspondents, we worked out of the Marine Combat Information Bureau (the CIB) in Da Nang. That was a place to get a hot shower, a hot meal, a cold drink, and a change of clothes after days in the field covering an operation. We'd make our way back to the CIB to file our stories and dispatch our film, but we seldom lingered long there.

The CIB was in an old motel the Marines had leased. It was built in the shape of a horseshoe with its open end on the Han River. News organizations, such as the AP, NBC, CBS, ABC, the *New York Times*, *Time* Magazine and others rented rooms there for correspondents. A bird colonel commanded the CIB and managed everything from getting the laundry done and feeding us, to providing news briefings and transportation for us.

Marines were assigned a variety of duties to make the CIB run, but managing a Vietnamese staff and caring for thirty or forty civilians was seldom smooth sailing. Consider the case of the warrant officer occasionally assigned to tend bar in the CIB dining room. One afternoon an Agence France-Presse (AFP) correspondent—one of the few female correspondents in Vietnam in 1966—sat down at the bar and ordered a martini. The warrant officer mixed gin with a whiff of dry vermouth, shook it with ice, and strained it into a glass. The correspondent, who later said she had been expecting a genteel glass of chilled dry vermouth, took a sip, wrinkled her nose and growled, "What the f— is this?"

Without thinking, the nonplussed warrant officer answered in kind: "It's a f—ing martini!"

With the warrant officer standing at attention in his office a short time later, the major who was XO of the CIB explained that's not the way a Marine speaks to a lady. I was grandly amused when, months later, after a lot of other Marines had encountered the correspondent's foul mouth, she was barred from Marine installations and operations because she talked too dirty.

Bob Bowen was a nice guy with a sense of humor in the midst of this chaotic scene, and when we had free time, we occasionally played pinochle. We were engaged in a game of three-handed, cutthroat pinochle with another correspondent in the AP room at the CIB late on the night the Vietcong first fired rockets at Da Nang Air Base. We hit the deck when the rockets began whistling overhead because initially we had no idea where they were going to land. But as the rockets began to slam into the air base and a civilian village beyond the base, we scrambled for information on the attack.

At 3 a.m., my bureau was closed for the night in Saigon, so I had a few hours to get my story together. But Bob wanted pictures and asked if he could borrow the aged and battered Jeep the AP rented from a local man. I pitched him the keys and he grabbed a camera.

Bob Bowen was above much of the hijinks correspondents get involved in on overseas assignments, especially in combat. He commanded respect from me and other correspondents because he was a nice guy, but he also was a squared-away Marine. He loved reporting on the successes of fellow Marines.

Covering the war was a seven-day-a-week job. I remember one Sunday afternoon I had an appointment to interview Lieutenant General Lewis W. Walt, commander of the III Marine Amphibious Force, which meant all the Marines in Vietnam. I had an escort from the CIB who insisted I be early for my appointment. But my scheduled time came and went with no general in sight.

I cooled my heels for another twenty minutes before the muscular, barrel-chested Lieutenant General Walt strode in and asked, "Bob, you want to talk or go to a fight?"

I figured there was only one reasonable answer. When I said I wanted to go to the fight, Lieutenant General Walt turned to an aide, and said, "Captain, take my chopper and take Bob down to Marble Mountain."

Let me tell you, when you fly into a Marine camp in a helicopter with three stars on the side, you get lots of attention. And the battle at Marble Mountain turned out to be the only firefight in the country that day, which allowed my story to lead the war roundup that day.

Later, when I told Bob Bowen what happened, he said I gave Lieutenant General Walt the right answer. Going to the fight was what Bob would have done if he had been in the same situation.

Bob Gassaway. Ph.D.
Professor Emeritus
Department of Communication and Journalism
University of New Mexico
Albuquerque, New Mexico

PREFACE

In 2010, I began to make good on a promise I had made to my friends who had asked that I write this book.

> *Bob—I have been looking at your postings on Facebook—photos, etc., and now wonder why you are not putting them together in a book,* One Marine's View of the Vietnam War—*and when it is done—I would like my copy signed.*
>
> George Lussier
> Former Virginia National Executive
> Committeeman of the American Legion

> *Bob, I love your Vietnam images. My son just marvels at them. Keep them coming! Any progress yet about a possible photo book?*
> Franklin Cox, U.S. Marine Vietnam Veteran
> Author of the award-winning *Lullabies for Lieutenants*

There were others, but I think you get the idea.

In 2011, I purchased an Apple iPad 2. It became my constant companion. In September 2013, I upgraded to the latest model iPad. Whenever a question comes up—on any subject—and I'm near a wireless network I can access, I can find an answer to the question. I even learned how to use the device lying on my side in bed. Eventually I developed a method of typing with one finger—actually the thumb on my right hand. I got pretty good at it—about thirty words a minute! When you consider this book contains more than seventy thousand words, you can hazard a guess as to how many times my thumb struck the keyboard of my iPad to type this manuscript.

In the final stages of writing the book, I discovered that writing on an iPad and converting it to Microsoft Word on a personal computer is extremely cumbersome, so I wrote the final six chapters on my laptop.

ACKNOWLEDGEMENTS

As noted in the Foreword, Bob Gassaway, Ph.D., is a retired Professor of Journalism and Communication at the University of New Mexico, Albuquerque. He is also a friend. Bob was a war correspondent for the Associated Press in Da Nang, Vietnam, when we first met in 1967. We crossed paths again in Miami in 1969. Bob was there with the AP. I was passing through Florida gathering material for stories for *Leatherneck* Magazine.

Three years later, in 1972, we met again in Columbia, Missouri. Bob was working for the Columbia *Daily Tribune*. He later earned his doctorate at the University of Missouri, Columbia, and taught journalism there for three years before moving to Albuquerque and joining the faculty of the Department of Communication and Journalism at the University of New Mexico. Affectionately known as Dr. Bob by many of his students, Gassaway retired from full-time teaching in 2006, but continued writing until his passing in May 2016. His review of my work and suggestions on ways to make it better in its early stage was of immense help.

Others who helped jog my memory or guided me through the publication labyrinth were Amy Marie Adams, Mawk Arnold, Jim Bathurst, Frank Beardsley, Rich Clarkson, Jack Corn, Franklin Cox, Dale Dye, Ed Evans, Bobby Garwood, Don Gilmore, John Hembrough, Rich Lavers, Jack Paxton, Sally Pritchett, Steve Stibbens, Paul Thompson, and Fred Tucker.

A special thanks to my editor, Robin Kern.

INTRODUCTION

I cannot recall ever wanting to be a fireman, a cop, a cowboy, a doctor, a lawyer, or any of those things most young boys aspire to being. My whole life has been devoted to communicating—writing, making photographs, reporting the news—be it printed or broadcast.

My friends have been urging me to write this book for a long time. I have always been a pack rat. I have notes, letters, and photographs covering my entire life—from birth to the present. This material was immensely helpful when I began writing the story of my life. Having "living" friends from my past that I could call on to jog my memory about some events was also nice.

CHAPTER 1

Growing Up in Norfolk, Virginia

*Young people are in a condition like
permanent intoxication because youth
is sweet and they are growing.*
~ Aristotle, 384 BC–322 BC

I can't say my youth was a hardscrabble existence, but there were many challenges.

For example, I've worked all my life. An early entry in my baby book, penciled in by Mom next to a steel 1943 penny Scotch-taped to the page, says, "Bobby's first money earned for helping rake the leaves—age two."

I raked a lot of leaves and cut a lot of grass before I reached age ten, earning between fifty and seventy-five cents a yard. That was in the day of push lawn mowers. I earned money by collecting newspapers and scrap metal. A neighborhood friend and I got his dad to drive us to the salvage yard where we'd sell the scrap by the pound. I also collected and washed used soft drink bottles and sold them for a penny apiece at the local grocery store.

I saw an ad on the back of a comic book looking for boys and girls to sell Cloverine Salve, a cure all for cuts, rashes, and a multitude of things that ailed you. I sent away for a supply and sold the magic ointment door-to-door one summer. Nothing escaped my moneymaking eye. I sold vegetable and flower seeds. Magazine subscriptions were on my list one summer, along with a paper route. I bagged groceries and carried them to cars for tips.

Mom took my sister, Dolores, and me to her hometown, Stanley, North Carolina, for two weeks each summer. Between swimming in the creek, eating watermelons and green apples, and getting reacquainted with all the cousins, I'd venture over to the local cemetery and collect the red ribbons on the flowers thrown away after they had served their usefulness. I used the ribbons to decorate pine boughs when December rolled around back home in Norfolk, Virginia. I'd sell the Christmas boughs in front of the Colonial grocery store in downtown Norview for twenty-five cents apiece. That earned me the money to buy Mom her traditional Christmas present, a potato peeler. I had given her a potato peeler years earlier and she gushed over it so much I decided to give her a new one each year. We had some good laughs over that in later years.

When I was twelve, I broke both bones in my right leg just above the ankle while sliding into second base during a recess softball game. We used a brick for the base. All of the anklebones were dislocated. That kept me out of school for a few weeks during which several friends brought me assignments so I could keep up with my studies. If that had happened today, an attorney would have come calling offering his or her services, and after paying an exorbitant fee, my family would have been living on easy street. My incident came during a simpler time, a time when you just picked yourself up, brushed yourself off, and started all over again.

One classmate brought me an old guitar. My dad bought some strings and I was beginning to make some progress until one day after school when a friend came running to say hello. I was on the breezeway. The guitar was lying on the concrete slab at my side. The friend's leap landed him smack-dab in the middle of the guitar. The guitar was totally useless after that and I never completed my lessons.

2

Recovering from broken leg, spring 1953.

A girl classmate, whose father worked for a jukebox distribution company, brought me several stacks of old 78 rpm country and western records. There were songs by Little Jimmy Dickens, Red Foley, Jimmy Rogers, Ernest Tubb, Hank Williams, and Kitty Wells to name a few. Foley's "Chattanooga Shoeshine Boy" became my first "earworm." When my leg healed, the song stayed with me and became the springboard for my first real job as a shoeshine boy at the local barbershop. As I shined the shoes, I'd pop the rag and sing the song.

When springtime rolled around, I'd head to the local strawberry farm at the corner of Bells Road (now Norview Avenue) and Military Highway. You could pick your own strawberries for ten cents a pint. I'd take them door-to-door and sell them for twenty-five cents a pint.

In the autumn preceding my thirteenth birthday, I discovered a "Fur-Fish-Game" magazine and became interested in muskrat trapping. There were a lot of muskrats, "swamp rabbits," in the marshes and lakes around Norfolk, so I scraped together enough money to buy four muskrat traps and set out to earn my first million. I chose the lakes on the east side of Military Highway as my principle trapping ground. I could get there in about fifteen minutes on my bicycle.

I checked my traps twice a day, when I came home from school and early in the morning before going to school. I skinned the muskrats I caught, stretched them on cedar shingles, scraped them and put them in the sun to dry. My buyer was Sears and Roebucks in Philadelphia. Depending on the color and quality of the pelt, I'd get from two to three dollars apiece. One especially dark morning I rode my bike to the lakes to check my traps. Fortunately, it was a Saturday. I would be there much longer than usual that morning. As I approached the location of one of my traps, I could hear a lot of thrashing in the water. I recalled seeing some persimmon seed droppings in the vicinity of where I'd set my trap the afternoon before, so I decided to wait until daybreak before approaching the animal that was making such a racket. Raccoons eat persimmons and they can be very mean when caught in a trap.

Preparing for ride to the lakes to check my muskrat traps, winter 1952–1953.

The thrashing stopped just before daybreak and I cautiously approached where I had set the trap. Much to my surprise, it was not a raccoon, but a large gray fox. My first thought was of the money I was about to earn. Then I thought of my mom. That fox skin would make a nice gift for her approaching birthday. She didn't have a fox shawl. Now she would.

I pedaled home as fast as I could with the gray fox draped over the handlebars. I must have started yelling before I rounded the corner of the street we lived on because when I turned into our driveway, Mom was standing on the porch wondering what all the commotion was about.

When she saw my prize and learned of my plans, she would have none of it. "This is your big day, Bobby," she said. "It's your chance to make some real money." So the decision was taken out of my hands. My gift of a fox shawl was rejected and I set about skinning my fox with all the care of a skilled surgeon. I was going to be rich!

The fox was skinned to perfection. No nicks anywhere in the skin. After it dried, I carefully wrapped the pelt in brown paper and sent it to Philadelphia. I was on pins and needles, as they say down south, until I received my payment from Sears and Roebucks—all fifteen cents of it!

There was an explanation with the check. It said fox fur was no longer in vogue. Fox fur was highly sought after in the 1930s and 1940s, but not the 1950s. I was disappointed. I earned more money for a good muskrat hide. My mom was devastated. "I could have been wearing a fox shawl made by my son," she'd say in later years as she recalled the event. I still have the invoice packed away somewhere. "One gray fox fur: 15 cents."

Claude Bice was my best friend in grade school. He arrived at midyear of the 6th grade. Our teacher was a country girl from Tennessee, Mrs. Harris. She interrupted her daily reading of Little Britches to us one day in January 1952 when the new kid arrived after transferring in from a Norfolk city school. We were in the county. Mrs. Harris asked him to tell us his name. He replied, "Claude Bice," ma'am, "but you can call me Sonny."

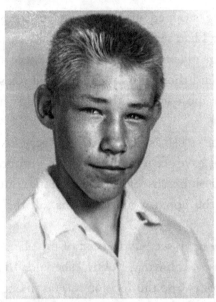

Claude "Sonny" Bice remains a close friend
after our initial meeting in the sixth grade, 1952.

I'm told I got my entrepreneurial spirit from my dad. He used to tell of swimming the Big Sandy River in Wayne County, West Virginia, as a boy. A farmer on the Kentucky side of the river grew the best watermelons. Dad would make the swim with a burlap sack in tow. He would put two watermelons into the sack and float back to the West Virginia side on his watermelon raft. He never said whether he made any money on his cross-river jaunts, so I guess he ate the ill-gotten gain.

The railroad stockyards in Huntington were another story. They held frequent swap shows there and as a young man, Dad was a regular visitor. One day he arrived with a broken Barlow knife in his pocket. After a succession of upgrade trades, he rode home on a swaybacked mule.

I was born in Huntington, West Virginia, on January 12, 1941. My dad worked there as an apprentice printer for the Huntington *Herald-Dispatch*. The newspaper threw the Union out shortly after my birth, and with a family in the making, Dad and Mom began a journey looking for permanent work. With war looming on the horizon, steady work was at a minimum. They made two stops in North Carolina, at High Point and Charlotte, before Dad heard about a job opening in Norfolk, Virginia.

My first set of wheels, Huntington, West Virginia, 1941.

We arrived in Norfolk in October 1942 and never moved again. That is, we never moved to another city. We moved nine times in Norfolk. Dad drew up plans for three homes he contracted to have built between 1942 and 1952. The others were rental homes. I was enrolled in eight different schools.

My dad served as a Civil Defense air raid warden during World War II. He would put on his helmet and walk his "beat," making sure the neighbors had their blinds shut tight during blackout warnings. Nazi U-boats were frequently sighted off the Tidewater Coast and Norfolk was right in the middle. Air raid warnings were frequent.

Dad's eye for ways to feed his family and make extra money "to make ends meet" never ceased to amaze me. Before she passed away in 2008 at age ninety-six, Mom described our early days in Norfolk, "In October 1942," she said, "a brand new, tiny little new cottage was up for rent. Never been lived in. Your dad got it for thirty-five dollars a month."

She said the cottage was twenty-five-feet long and sixteen-feet wide. It had a seven-feet-wide living room, a tiny bath with the "cutest little short tub," two bedrooms, and a kitchen six-feet wide. There was no hot water, no kitchen cabinets, no wiring for an electric range, and no oven. The home was not piped for gas. Mom said we were so lucky to get it! My dad, Tommy, found a little electric thing that Mom could cook on and bake in. Our landlord loaned us a hot plate. Mom heated with a coal Heatrola, so in the winter she could heat water on it or boil things.

Mom went on to explain how she and Dad supplemented his meager wages as a printer. "There was a vacant lot across the street and we got permission to garden it. I grew vegetables, picked blackberries, and canned them."

Wednesday was my dad's day off. Mom called it Dad's fishing day. Mom said, "One time I would go with him and Tommy, Jr. [my half-brother] would stay with Bobby [me]. The next week I would stay home. Mostly, we would go out in a rowboat at Ocean View, but I would get motion sickness. I finally had to give it up. We canned the large croakers in a hot bath cooker. Tommy took some to his mother in West Virginia by train."

"We had a little shed in the back yard," Mom said. "We put our laundry heater there, and that is where I did my canning. Dad also built a chicken house. We had baby chicks to raise for layers. They grew to be big hens and laid big white eggs." Occasionally Mom would let me feed them.

One of my early family chores was feeding the chickens we raised in our backyard on Harrell Avenue, Norfolk, Virginia. 1943.

Growing up in the city of Norfolk and later Norview, a section of Norfolk County, was full of adventures and excitement. One spring day in 1949, while searching for frog eggs in the ditch alongside our home on the corner of Alexander and Strand Streets, I spotted a huge black snake—must have been five feet long—warming itself on the edge of the pavement. As quick as a flash, I raced home to get a jar to put the snake in when I captured it.

I threw open the kitchen door and rushed to the cabinet beneath the sink. Mom always had a few large empty jars there. "What in the world are you doing?" Mom said. "There's a snake on the street." I said." Before I could say anything else, Mom flew out the door, grabbed the hoe leaning against the porch railing, and went searching for the snake.

When I arrived with a jar to put "my" snake in, Mom was beaming from ear to ear. The snake lay at her feet in four or five pieces. "Don't worry," she said, "I killed it." Mom hated snakes.

One morning in the winter of 1950–1951, I fell down the stairs at our house on Elmhurst Street. The doctor was called. A trip to the hospital followed and I was discovered to have a bleeding duodenal ulcer. Ten years old and an ulcer! I was in the DePaul Hospital for about two weeks. Seven blood transfusions and a diet of whole milk and belladonna brought me back to health and I resumed my otherwise normal childhood.

Normal, that is except that Dad would not let me play football following that incident. The boys on the block had played a game of tackle in a vacant lot the day before I fell down the steps. Dad couldn't accept the fact that a bleeding ulcer had caused me to fall. He blamed it on the football game. When junior high school arrived, I was relegated to being a water boy to earn my football letter, complete with an "M" for manager woven into the blue and white "N" for Norview.

One Sunday that year, after coming home from church, Mom began rushing to make her usual family dinner. But, it was not a good day. During the rush to make fresh biscuits from scratch, something Mom could do with ease blindfolded, she forgot an ingredient. The biscuits were hard as rocks.

Family portrait, Christmas 1950. Mom and Dad,
brother, Tom, and sister, Dolores.

My sister and I said nothing, but Dad was not as polite. He let it be known that his biscuit was too hard to eat. Mom promptly stood up, grabbed the biscuit bowl, collected those on mine and my sister's plate, then my dad's, and went to the back door, opened it, and pitched them out.

The family dog, bounded over, sniffed, picked a biscuit up in his mouth and walked to the garden's edge where he promptly dug a hole, dropped the biscuit in, covered it, and walked back to the rest of the biscuits to get another one. We watched out the dining room window as the dog repeated the process until all of the biscuits had been buried.

We held back our laughter as long as we could, but eventually it burst forth in all our youthful glee. Even Dad chuckled a little, though he tried hard not to.

Mom simply straightened her proud back and in her firmest Scotch-Irish voice said, "Well, at least a dog knows a good thing when he sees it. Dogs always bury their prized food to eat later, you know."

Later that year, Dad came home from work one day with a pair of tickets to an upcoming baseball game. The Norfolk Tars, a minor league team in the Yankee farm system, was having an especially good year in 1951. I don't remember who the Tars were playing, or whether they won the game, but they finished the season with a record of 81-58 and won the Piedmont League by 33 percentage points. The manager was Mayor Smith. The star player was Bill "Moose" Skowron, who later played for the Yankees.

Dad had bought a Rawlings baseball and brought it to the game. At some point, he passed it to the dugout with a note requesting it be signed by all of the players. They obliged, and I treasured that ball and showed it to visitors until the time I had children and they decided they needed a ball to play with. The autographed ball was soon unreadable. I haven't the slightest idea whatever became of it.

As the years went by and my body healed fully and attained "working" size, Dad's "get rich schemes" always involved me.

Our home in Norview in 1952 was built on a one-acre lot. Half of the lot was wooded. When Dad decided he was going to raise and sell azalea plants, I got the job of clearing the center portion of the backyard. This meant cutting down the trees, removing and burning the stumps, and cultivating the land so Mom and Dad could plant the young seedlings.

We didn't sell many azaleas, and despite my labors, I never got any of the proceeds. There were still a few azaleas blooming in the back woods when Mom sold the house in the 1980s.

I also didn't get any of the money my dad earned selling worms. I was heavily involved in that backbreaking venture. It involved digging three holes, six-feet long, three-feet wide and three-feet deep. Each hole was lined with two-by-twelve boards, wedged to stay in place.

The dirt I dug from the holes was cleared of all roots by sifting through a homemade sieve. The dirt fell back into the hole as I sifted it. When a hole was three-quarters full, I added peat moss to bring it to ground level. I used a garden cultivator (forked hoe) to combine the peat moss and the dirt.

After the worm beds were built, Dad sent away for a supply of red earthworms. We divided them equally among the three beds. We moistened the soil and sprinkled a mixture of chicken mash on top of each bed. That's what the worms ate.

To enhance the prospect of selling his worms, Dad produced an ink blotter which I distributed to local hardware stores and other places where fishing supplies were sold. Dad was known as the "Bard of the Composing Room" at the Norfolk Newspapers, Inc., where he worked as a Linotype operator.

The blotter's message, along with our address.

With wormy wigglers as your bait
You won't have to sit and wait
For anything that wears a fin
Wormy wigglers lure them in.

Unfortunately, the catchy ditty on the blotter didn't lure many fishermen our way and along with the azaleas, the wormy wigglers were alive and well when Mom moved thirty years later.

There would be a time in the future that I would again resort to manual labor to earn a salary. But, I was still a student in the 1950s and it was while a student that I began focusing on journalism. Even without putting a name on my focus, I was drawn to writing and reporting what I saw around me. My dad said I had printer's ink in my blood.

CHAPTER 2

Printer's Ink in My Blood

*It was while making newspaper deliveries, trying to miss the bushes and hit
the porch, that I first learned the importance of accuracy in journalism.*
~ Charles Osgood TV Commentator

My journalistic journey began in the seventh grade when I won a
Quill & Scroll award for an essay I wrote and read aloud during a
special program in the auditorium with parents invited. The essay
was titled "My Community and I." It described the deplorable state of
affairs in the Norfolk community of Norview, through the eyes of a
twelve-year-old.

I wrote about how the store owners on Sewells Point Road would
sweep out their stores onto the sidewalks, then wash the sidewalks
down with a garden hose. This attracted rats that would scurry about
the open street gutters eating any bits of food they could find. My
essay described the open garbage cans behind the grocery store, full
of rotting produce, which also attracted rats.

The essay was written on three-by-five-inch cards. I still have the
essay and the Quill & Scroll lapel pin I received for my effort. I also
received a miniature camera with the suggestion that I document my
findings for any future "tell all" essays, but I don't recall ever taking a
photo with the tiny dime-store toy camera.

My first camera. It was busted; didn't work,
but who cared? I was a photographer!

Mom and Dad encouraged my writing. Mom bought me a secondhand R. C. Allen typewriter. My dad, a Linotype operator with typing skills equal to about one hundred words a minute, heard me hunting and pecking on the typewriter one day when he came home from work and let me know I was demonstrating solid typing skills. I never did learn the "touch typing" method, but my hunt-and-peck skills eventually reached seventy-five words a minute.

A lot of my senior teen years were spent with the Methodist Youth Fellowship organization of my church. Keeping to my chosen profession, I served as the district publicity officer. I wrote the monthly newsletter, typed it on a stencil, and printed it on the church mimeograph machine. I also wrote press releases about youth fellowship programs and upcoming meetings and submitted them to the Norfolk *Ledger-Dispatch* for publication. My first effort to publicize the newly elected slate of district officers, was published in the summer of 1959.

I spent my eighteenth summer as a day laborer for local construction companies. By the time September arrived, my hands were rough and callused from digging foundations, cutting and nailing lumber, tying rebar, and pouring and finishing concrete floors. The money was good and the exercise was just what a growing teenager needed, but it would not be my life's work.

In August 1959, I boarded a train in Norfolk, along with several other members of the MYF, and began the eight hundred twenty-one-mile trip to Purdue University in Lafayette, Indiana, for the National Convocation of Methodist Youth. The weekend program featured former First Lady Eleanor Roosevelt, jazz pianist Dave Brubeck, jazz vibraphonist Lionel Hampton, and singer Odetta, often referred to as the voice of the civil rights movement.

New officers of the Norfolk MYF District, 1959.
Front Row (l-r): Helen Hurt, Ann Daniels, Doug Davidson, Frances Wellons.
Back Row (l-r): Butch Morgan, Patsy Wickers, Pat Thomas,
Virginia Gatlin, Bob Bowon.

The personnel director for the Norfolk newspaper was a member of my church. My dad, recently deceased, had been a Linotype operator at the newspaper. So it was only natural that when I decided to pursue my life's work, I would apply for work at the Norfolk Newspapers, Inc.

Entry level for me was as a mail clerk, an ideal position for a hard-charging young man trying to launch his career. As mail clerk, I met all of the senior officers and managers on a daily basis. Within four months I had transferred to the *Ledger-Dispatch* newsroom as a copyboy. I can still hear the sound of "Copeeee" as a reporter would call out to announce he or she had a story for a copyboy to pick up and take to an editor at the front of the newsroom.

First job at Norfolk Newspapers, Inc., as mail clerk, 1959.

Political correctness arrived at the Norfolk newspapers in the late 1950s and overnight, copyboys were editorial assistants. This would prove to be one of the biggest breaks of my life.

The newsroom editors then were the Reilly brothers, Charles and Tom, Clarence Walton, and Turner Dozier, the sports editor. Walton and Dozier were my favorites. Walton was instrumental in getting me promoted to chief copyboy (chief editorial assistant) after a few months on the job and Dozier gave me the chance to write for publication.

When I approached Dozier about some freelance sports writing assignments, he asked, "Can you write?" A natural question, but despite my assurances that I could, he gave me an assignment to write a hypothetical story about a high school football game. He evidently liked what I wrote, but nonetheless bled all over the copy with his red ink editing pen and had me write it again.

A few more red-inked submissions and Dozier rewarded me with a ticket to cover the Norview High School football team in a home game against Suffolk High. The Norview Pilots, led by halfback Eddie Versprille, defeated the Suffolk Red Raiders, 33–13.

I was so impressed with Versprille's performance that night—two, back-to-back sixty-four-yard touchdowns on the ground and one touchdown pass—that I began sending weekly newspaper clippings of Versprille's performance to the Wigwam Wisemen of America, sponsor of an annual national All-America high school football team.

Norview High ended the season undefeated with a record of 10–0 and Eddie won a spot on the second place All-America team that year. Sports columnist John Crittenden wrote in his "In Brief" column, "Give young Bob Bowen a big assist on Eddie Versprille's All-American selection." Crittenden said Versprille surely deserved the award, ". . . but might not have been recognized except for Bowen's devotion to daily duty."

I had bylines in the sports section of the *Ledger-Dispatch* throughout the rest of 1959, "Norview Cheerleaders Work Hard to Boost School Spirit," "Defense Outgains Norview's Offense." In the newspaper's feature section, "Double Casting 'Menagerie' Will Be Finale for Director," an article about a high school drama teacher.

In October and November, most of my Thursday nights were spent at the Norfolk Arena, the venue for the weekly professional wrestling program. So, from writing a hypothetical report of a high school football game, I went to writing factual reports of quasi-sports events.

A headline in October 1959 said "Gals Belong Home Says Pro Wrestler." The headline quoted Ike Eakins, a former pro football player and soldier turned professional wrestler. He was referring to one of the headliners that night, Slave Girl Moolah. The bill also featured an eight-man free for all with Eakins, George Becker, Tito Carron, Cyclone Anaya, Larry Hamilton, Charley Laye, Ted Christy, and Prince

Omar throwing bodies all over and out of the ring. What more could a young aspiring writer ask for—bodies being thrown everywhere and the opportunity to write about it.

Clifton Guthrie, a *Ledger-Dispatch* photographer, accompanied me on most of these assignments. I can't recall us ever discussing an approach to covering an event, be it high school football or professional wrestling. He knew what he had to do and I knew my role.

Two of my favorite pro wrestling events involved Ricki Starr and Haystack Calhoun. Starr studied music and drama at Purdue University, West Lafayette, Indiana, but when it came time to get a job, he donned a tutu and ballet slippers and climbed into the professional wrestling ring. My story of his appearance at the Norfolk Arena in November 1959, read "Ballet is Equalizer, Says Wrestler."

Haystack Calhoun also appeared at the Arena in November 1959. The headline for my bylined article read "Haystack Gets Paid For Fun." When he plopped his six hundred and one-pound body onto Ted Christy, his opponent, Haystack was the only one having any fun.

To explain his weight, Haystack admitted eating a dozen eggs for breakfast along with two pounds of bacon, one pan of biscuits, and drinking a half-gallon of milk. His supper included "three to five pounds of meat and a carload of vegetables." He skipped lunch; otherwise he might have weighed more than six hundred and one pounds.

I was so pleased with my progress as a "cub reporter," that I approached City Editor Clarence Walton and asked about a full-time reporting position on the newspaper staff. As gently as he could, he explained that "in the old days" I would have met the qualifications for such a promotion, but in the world that existed then, I needed a college degree to be a reporter. I was crushed. My family had no money to pay for college tuition, I knew nothing about applying for a scholarship, and the fifty dollars a week I made at the newspaper, before taxes, left nothing for a college fund.

The very next day I applied for an apprenticeship as a Linotype machinist in the Norfolk Newspapers Composing Room. I continued working at the newspaper, and while not a member of the reporting staff, I continued to solicit freelance assignments from the Sports Department.

I worked as an apprentice Linotype machinist through June of 1960. I began each day by cleaning space bands. They were inserted into a line of type matrices to justify the proper column width before sending it to the molding disk where hot lead was injected to produce a finished line of type. Invariably, some of the space bands would be contaminated with the hot lead and before they could be used again, they had to be cleaned.

Linotype spacebands and a line of type.

Cleaning space bands was no fun. It involved rubbing them on a smooth surface in a mixture of fine graphite powder. The mixture was especially designed for cleaning space bands made by the Mergenthaer Linotype Company. The space band was considered clean when the wedge shaped insert would move freely the length of the band. The graphite powder penetrated the pores in my hands and it took a long time to clean them with borax soap.

CHAPTER 3

The Marine Corps Calls

*A Marine is a Marine . . . . there's no such thing as a former Marine. You're
a Marine, just in a different uniform and you're in a different phase of your
life. But, you'll always be a Marine because you went to Parris Island, San
Diego or the hills of Quantico. There's no such thing as a former Marine.*
~ General James F. Amos,
35th Commandant of the Marine Corps

In early July 1960, I began making the rounds of the armed forces
recruiting offices in the federal building housing the post office across
the street from the newspaper offices. My brother had served in the Air
Force, so I checked with that recruiter first. No quotas available. Same
story with the Army. Norfolk is a Navy town and having seen sailors
every day of life, I passed on checking with the petty officer manning
the Navy office.

A master sergeant was at the desk when I walked into the Marine
Corps recruiting office. "Sit down, son," he said. "Why do you want
to be a Marine?" My reply came as a surprise. Becoming a Marine was
not a lifelong desire. No one in my family had ever served in the Corps.
"Well, the Army and Air Force don't need anyone right now and I don't
want to be a sailor."

Rejecting the Navy out of hand pleased the master sergeant and he
reached for some papers and said, "Here. Fill these out." I enlisted for
four years, and on July 28, I was on a train from Norfolk to Richmond,

Virginia, where I would be given a physical. If I passed the test, I would be on the next train to Parris Island, South Carolina, by way of Yemassee, the principle railroad head for South Carolina's Lowcountry.

The certificate hanging on my wall today tells the story.

> *This is to certify that Robert Lee Bowen has successfully passed the required mental, moral and physical examinations and has been accepted for enlistment in the United States Marine Corps. The defense of our country and our freedoms is the duty and privilege of every citizen. The Marine Corps has a proud tradition of outstanding service to our country in peace and war. Voluntary enlistment in this elite military organization is a clear demonstration of these American qualities of patriotism and loyalty to God and country.*
>
> Major Harold Hatch
> Officer in Charge of the Marine Corps Recruiting
> Station in Richmond

Before boarding the train in Norfolk, Sports Editor Dozier and I went to lunch at a small sandwich shop on Granby Street. It was a nice farewell lunch. Dozier picked up the tab and said he would have some freelance sports writing assignments for me if my experiment with the Marines didn't work out.

Much has been written about the Marine Corps boot camp at Parris Island, South Carolina, but every Marine has his own memories of his time there and I'm no different. My senior drill instructor was Staff Sergeant Jimmie D. Marion, a Korean War veteran from Alabama. The junior DIs were Staff Sergeant R. G. Morella and Sergeant J. G. Burke. 1st Lieutenant J. S. Ficken was the series officer. They were responsible for molding the herd of misfits that descended on them that summer into a cohesive group of men who thought and acted as a unit.

From (l-r): senior drill instructor SSgt Jimmie Marion,
JDIs Sgt J. D. Burke and SSgt R. J. Morella.

About the time we arrived at Parris Island, the Marine Corps decided to change its drill from eight-man squad to thirteen-man squad. While the emphasis was on thirteen-man squad's drill for our platoon, we also learned eight-man squad's drill. We spent what seemed like endless days drilling on the huge parade field, affectionately known as the "Grinder."

Platoon 171 on the Grinder during final field day.

Drill accomplishes two things. It gets a group of people from point A to point B in an orderly fashion and in the shortest amount of time. It also teaches discipline and how to give and take orders.

Each drill instructor had his own distinctive drill voice and his cadence was something he developed over time and with much practice. I can still hear SSgt Marion calling cadence. In future years when I had the opportunity to drill troops, I used a modified version of his cadence. Some things are hard to forget.

We were issued tie-ties when we arrived at Parris Island. We did our own laundry and the tie-ties were used to tie our clothes to dry on the line. Smokers were permitted to carry their cigarette packs in their socks. It was not unusual to end a laundry day with a DI saying, "If you've got 'em, smoke 'em," meaning if you smoked and had a cigarette you could now smoke. When you finished you had to "field strip" what was left of the cigarette and scatter the tobacco in the air. The paper that was left would be tightly rolled into a ball, slipped into your pocket, and later discarded in a trash can.

As a smoker, I enjoyed these opportunities to do something different than the routine training. Some recruits started smoking in boot camp, just to take advantage of the privilege.

The platoon was organized into squads and fireteams. Fireteams were assigned guard duty to make sure the squad bay was secure during "lights out." One night my fireteam was assigned this duty and as the fire team leader, my position was in the DI's office. Around midnight, the door swung open and there stood SSgt Marion. I was looking at the newspaper he'd left open on his desk. "Just what do you think you're doing recruit?" the senior DI asked.

"Looking at the newspaper, Sir."

With that, SSgt Marion began his lecture on Marines and newspapers. Marines had no need to read the newspaper, he said. If we needed to know anything about what was going on in the world, our officers—noncommissioned officers or the Commandant himself— would tell us what we needed to know. At best, the only thing we might want to read each day was the obituary page. That would let us know when a senior Marine in our occupational specialty had passed away, thereby increasing our chance for future promotion. I've never forgotten that impromptu lecture.

Our platoon provided the Corps with sixty-eight new Marines, a title we were not permitted to use until we graduated. We would have had more, but a few fell out along the way for a variety of reasons.

One afternoon we were sitting on our footlockers dissembling and cleaning our bayonets. Suddenly, screams came from the other end of the squad bay. One of the recruits had put his left hand on top of his foot locker and was repeatedly stabbing it with his bayonet. Recruits nearby quickly subdued him. Military police and an ambulance were called. The wounded recruit was whisked away and we never saw him again.

There were a few other incidents at Parris Island I need to mention before graduating and moving on to advanced combat training at Camp Geiger.

Claude "Sonny" Bice was one of my best friends in the 6th and 7th grades. As most school friendships go, time passes and old friends become memories. On our first day of physical exercise training at Parris Island, I was reunited with Sonny. He was a lance corporal, assigned as a physical education instructor. He came into view as I lowered myself on the pull-up bar. I wanted to jump down, grab him, and shake his hand. When our eyes locked, his stern look brought me to my senses and I let the moment pass. I did not see him again while in boot camp. (I learned later that he transferred to another East Coast command the following month). However, our paths crossed again several times during our careers.

Early in our training, the recruits of Platoon 171, 1st Battalion, 1st Marine Recruit Regiment, took a battery of tests, both physical and mental. We were also asked a series of questions designed to reveal where our interests lay and what work experience we had. Again, I passed the physical test with flying colors. I scored 128 on the standard GCT (General Classification Test), designed to determine one's ability to perform a myriad of jobs.

Questions about my employment history produced the fact that I had spent one summer of my youth as a laborer, I had worked as a mail clerk, I had written sports for a daily newspaper, I had cleaned spacebands in a newspaper's composing room, and I had worked as the chief editorial assistant for the Norfolk Newspapers, Inc.

In the final stages of boot camp, I qualified on the rifle range as an expert shooter with the M1 Garand rifle, despite never having fired a rifle before arriving at Parris Island. And, by qualifying as an expert rifleman, I joined a few others who also shot expert, for another week at the rifle range to receive training and to qualify with the .45 caliber pistol. I qualified as a marksman with the pistol.

Platoon 171 was billeted in an old wooden barracks. In late August, Hurricane Donna began churning up the Atlantic Ocean. Before long, Parris Island was in the storm's crosshairs.

Recruits in wooden buildings were relocated to brick barracks of the 3rd Regiment. Much of the storm's strength was spent in Florida, but folks in Beaufort County, South Carolina, lost homes, trees, piers, power lines, and crops. Donna remains the ninth largest hurricane ever recorded in the United States, causing twenty-six billion, eight hundred thousand dollars in damages.

One of the many highlights of our twelve-week training program at Parris Island was the five-mile forced march to Elliott's Beach and our overnight bivouac there. We learned how to pitch our tents. Each man carried one half of a tent which he'd combine with the shelter half another recruit carried. After pitching our tents, we ate cold C-rations.

Our C-rations were old. Most were Korean War vintage, but some had been boxed up during World War II. Mine were of the World War II vintage and contained little chocolate patties and what we called "John Wayne" crackers. The chocolate was good, but it gave me a severe case of the trots. On the march back to Mainside the following day I soon used up all the toilet paper provided in my C-ration box and I resorted to using Spanish moss which hung abundantly from the live oaks that lined the unpaved road we were on. The itching started quickly and my backside was burning up with a rash. The hike home was sheer torture. Lesson learned: never wipe your butt with Spanish moss.

A few days before final review and graduation in October, we learned who had earned coveted promotions to private first class and where we would be going after infantry training in North Carolina.

Group graduation photo.

I was not one of the lucky few who earned a PFC stripe, but I had been assigned the military occupational specialty (MOS) of 4300, basic information specialist, and my first duty station would be the Marine Corps Schools, Quantico, Virginia. Having been a chief editorial assistant at the Norfolk Newspapers was paying off big time. I was about to become a Marine Corps reporter!

I had become good friends with W. W. "Bill" Goodchild of Ohio. When graduation day neared, we introduced our moms to one another by mail. They exchanged letters and decided to drive down and attend our graduation.

My mom, Mary Ella, did not drive so Bill's mom, Madge, drove from Salem, Ohio, to Norfolk, Virginia, picked up my mom, then continued the grueling drive down U.S. Route 13 to Parris Island. They enjoyed our final parade and the graduation ceremony. We enjoyed showing them all the places we'd been during our training including the confidence course—especially the "slide for life"—the rifle range, and Elliott's Beach. I didn't say a word about the Spanish moss.

Elliott's Beach palm tree on graduation day.

We were among the last Marines to wear the beloved globe and anchor emblem on our shirt collars. Being able to wear the globe and anchor on the collar was an honor bestowed on Marines during World War I by Franklin D. Roosevelt, then Assistant Secretary of the Navy.

My boot camp photo.

Marines wore Army uniforms during World War I and during an after-battle visit to Belleau Wood, France, Roosevelt declared that henceforth all enlisted Marines would wear the emblem of Marines on their shirt collar. But, because it "made holes in the collar" the 22nd Commandant of the Marine Corps, General David M. Shoup, decided they would be worn no more. My recruit platoon graduation photograph shows us with the emblems on, and we left the base and checked into Camp Geiger wearing them, but we were not wearing them when we left there.

Camp Geiger is located on the Marine Corps' sprawling Camp Lejeune on North Carolina coast next door to Jacksonville. That's where we learned the basic skills of a Marine for duty in combat, small unit tactics, how to dig a latrine, how to make C-rations edible, how to throw a grenade, and about the finer points of being a rifleman, something all Marines are regardless of their MOS.

I also learned that not all Marines are "squared away"—regardless of their rank. We celebrated the 185th Marine Corps birthday while going through Infantry Training Regiment at Camp Geiger. We lived in Quonset huts and the company offices were in Quonset huts. We fell out and formed up in front of Company Headquarters the morning of November 10th, the Marine Corps birthday.

The Company gunnery sergeant "gunny" walked out of his office. He commanded, "At ease," read aloud a message Major General John A. Lejeune had directed be read to all Marines in 1921, and then read the current Commandant's birthday message. With the pomp and ceremony of the occasion over, he raised a leg, placed it on one of the wooden four-by-fours that held the white chain lining the walkway to the office and reached for a cigarette. He was wearing purple argyle socks!

I learned the basic skills of a Marine rifleman, NOT to wear purple socks in uniform, and left ITR with the stripe of a private first class on my sleeve. I had received a meritorious promotion based on my performance at ITR. My seventy-eight dollar monthly pay was about to increase to eighty-five dollars and fifty cents. I had nineteen days of leave at home in Norfolk before it was time to board a Greyhound bus for Triangle, the small town on U.S. Route 1 outside the massive Quantico Marine Corps Base. The date was December 6, 1960.

CHAPTER 4

Quantico

*The Marines I have seen around the world have
the cleanest bodies, the filthiest minds, the highest
morale, and the lowest morals of any group
of animals I have ever seen. Thank God for the
United States Marine Corps!*

~ Eleanor Roosevelt

Marine Corps Base, Quantico, VA, logo.

I was pleasantly surprised as I arrived at Marine Corps Base, Quantico "Crossroads of the Marine Corps" and the taxi wound its way up Fuller Road. It drove past the immaculate fairways and greens of the Medal of Honor Golf Course, through the main gate adjacent to the massive printing plant built in 1919, and on down tree-lined Barnett Avenue to D Building, home of Casual Company. That's where everyone reported when arriving for duty. Everything I saw told me I was on a college or university campus. I was going to journalism school!

The sergeant on duty endorsed my orders at 3:50 p.m. and set me straight in a heartbeat. I was not going to school. There was no journalism school at Quantico. The next morning I would report to Lejeune Hall as part of the cleaning crew. That's what new lower-ranked enlisted arrivals did at Quantico. They worked at mundane, but necessary, chores.

Lejeune Hall was where Lieutenant General Edward W. Snedeker, Commandant of Marine Corps Schools, and his staff, had their offices. The Informational Services Office was in the basement of the building's south wing. And that's where I was assigned to sweep and swab the corridor on the second day of my tour of duty at Quantico.

When I arrived to begin my work the next morning, Gunnery Sergeant Dick Arnold, editor of the Quantico *Sentry* newspaper, was already at his desk. He motioned for me to come into his office. "What's your name, Marine?" Before I could answer, "What's your MOS?"

When I told him my MOS was 4300, he got a smile on his face and reached for the phone. "You belong to me," he said. His call was to the company gunnery sergeant of Casual Company. After a brief conversation he told me to finish my work in the corridor, go to lunch, see the company gunny, and report back to him the following morning. That afternoon I relocated to Headquarters Company in A Building, and the following morning I reported to Gunny Arnold in ISO. Two women Marines were in charge of the office, 1st Lieutenant. Barbara J. Kessee was the Officer in Charge. The Assistant OIC was 2nd Lieutenant Barbara J. Roy. In addition to Gunny Arnold, the office was staffed by Master Sergeant Krichbaum, Gunnery Sergeant Ruby Maxwell, Staff Sergeants Ray Gilliland and Glen Ritchie, Corporals Dick Tulisiak and Jim Wooten, and Lance Corporal Ron Meyer.

My published sports writing for the Norfolk Newspapers was looked upon favorably and I was assigned duties as Quantico's sports publicist. The base sponsored two major sports events each year, the Quantico Track and Field Relays and the Christmas Basketball Tournament. Both events drew from colleges and universities up and down the East Coast. The varsity teams provided great publicity for the Corps and served as big recruiting draws for young men and women still in college.

Publicity for Quantico's varsity football program was handled by Cpl Tulisiak. Over the three-year period from 1959–1961, the team had a record of 29–6. Major Wil Overgaard was the team's coach during that period. Quantico defeated McClelland Air Force Base 90–0 in the Shrimp Bowl in Galveston, Texas, in 1959 to claim the All-Service title.

The Quantico *Sentry* newspaper was published every Friday. Each Thursday a few of us would accompany Gunny Arnold to the *Mercury Press* plant in Washington, D.C., where the newspaper was printed. There, we would proofread all of the galley sheets to ensure there were no errors when the newspaper arrived at Quantico the following morning for distribution.

The first time I made the trip was my first ever visit to the Nations' Capitol. I was particularly aghast at signs that said "No Standing." I had never seen that traffic sign before. The thought of a person not being able to stand on the sidewalk in Washington, D.C., was hard for me to understand. Learning that the sign was a warning for drivers to not stop and leave their cars was nice to know, but nonetheless an embarrassment for this young "country bumpkin."

Marines at Quantico were still puffing their chests with pride in the winter of 1960–1961 over the performance of one of their own that previous summer at the Rome Olympics. Sergeant Percy Price had defeated Cassius Clay in a preliminary bout to earn a spot on the USA team as its heavyweight entry. Price retired from the Corps as a master sergeant in 1976 after serving two tours in Vietnam. Clay changed his name to Mohamed Ali and you know the rest of that story. Two of Quantico's track and field athletes were also on the USA's 1960 Olympic team, 1,500 meter runner Lt Pete Close and shot putter Al Cantello.

Seven college teams joined the Quantico Marines in the basketball tournament in 1960, American University, Atlantic Christian (now Barton University), Belmont Abbey, Buffalo University, Jacksonville University, Philadelphia Textile (now Philadelphia University), and St. Michael's College. Belmont Abbey and Quantico met in the finals. The Marines won 85–62.

Press card.

The basketball tournament was not all we had on our plate that month. Quantico was hit with the first of three severe snowstorms that would not end until after the inauguration of President John F. Kennedy on January 20, 1961. As much as seventy cumulative inches of snow fell from Virginia to Maine in December, January, and February.

Wildlife was hit especially hard. With the ground covered with frozen snow, the deer, ducks, and geese along the Potomac River could not get food, so the Marines at Quantico came to the rescue. One day in February 1961, I was temporarily cut loose from my sports duties and boarded a helicopter to report on Marines dropping corn on frozen fields on the east side of the Potomac in Maryland. It was my first flight in any kind of aircraft. Exhilarating!

Marines of HMX-1, the helicopter squadron that flies the President of the United States, dropped thirty-six thousand pounds of corn on the more than eleven thousand acres of frozen swamp land in the Blackwater National Game Refuge. My report was on the front page of the Quantico *Sentry* weekly newspaper.

With Operation Corn Cob completed and reported on, I returned to my sports desk, where a full schedule of varsity basketball games, boxing matches, bowling, shooting matches, track and field, and other lesser events awaited my attention.

Quantico had a double-decker Scenicruiser that was used to transport it's sports teams up and down the East Coast for "away" competitions. When the basketball team hit the road, so did I. My job, in addition to writing about the games, was to serve as the traveling public relations man. Occasionally I would keep the team statistics. When games were carried on local radio stations, I would sit behind a microphone and provide color for the broadcast.

During the two seasons I traveled with the basketball team, we visited Mitchell Air Force Base on Long Island, Fort Dix in New Jersey, Fort Devens in Massachusetts, Fort Lee and the Navy in Virginia, Duquesne University in Pittsburgh, Holy Cross in Massachusetts, West Point in New York, the New York City Athletic Club, and Providence College in Rhode Island, to name but a few.

Each day, before boarding the bus, Captain Earl Rottsalk, the team coach, would give each of us two dollars. That was for our first meal, which we'd get at our first stop, normally a hamburger, hot dog or a sandwich, and a soda. This was repeated three times a day. Doesn't sound like much today, but at six dollars a day, if we had ever been on the road for a full month, the daily food stipend would have totaled $180.00. My monthly pay for much of 1961 was less than eight-six dollars a month.

Reporting duties were a mixed bag in 1961. In addition to sports, I was called on to write about the base dental facilities, a youth fishing tournament, a reserve unit's active duty training project, how the base high school was implementing the President's Youth Physical Fitness Program, the aircraft engineering squadron at Quantico's Air Station, and assorted other subjects. It was an assignment a young aspiring reporter would give his eye teeth for.

One spring day I was assigned to meet a group of newly arrived Marines who had been chosen to become officers through the Meritorious Noncommissioned Officer Program. My job was to get each Marine to fill out a Fleet Hometown News form. These forms were attached to a cover story describing the program, how a Marine was selected, and when they would graduate. All of that information was sent to the Fleet Hometown News Center at Great Lakes Naval Training Center in Chicago, Illinois. There, writers took the basic story, inserted the name and brief biographical information provided by each Marine, and sent it to each Marine's hometown newspaper.

When I opened the door to the barracks being used by the Marines attending the program, the man to my immediate left jumped to his feet, stood at attention, and said in a loud voice, "Well, I guess the shoe is on the other foot now, Sir." The Marine was Sgt J. G. Burke, one of my two boot camp junior drill instructors. He thought I was one of the Marines assigned to put the prospective officers through their paces. I just stared at him. "No," I said to myself "but I wish I were."

Life was never dull at Quantico. One day, Cpl Tulisiak was called to the base military police office. His wife had been pulled over and escorted to the MP office for failing to stop when a Marine was walking across Barnett Avenue to the PX (Post Exchange) in Little Hall. Cpl Tulisiak was fuming. "Haven't I told you time and time again that you always stop for troops in a clearly marked walkway?" "There were no troops," she recanted tactfully. "There was only one Marine."

Quantico was home for the Research and Development Command in the early 1960s. It is now the Marine Corps Systems Command. Secret contingency planning and equipment innovations take place there. As a result, the photo lab does a lot of highly classified photography at Quantico. This required an armed guard on duty at the lab to make sure those photographs remained secure. One night, the corporal assigned guard duty couldn't resist "slapping leather" with his Colt .45 when "Gunsmoke" came on the television. The corporal beat Matt Dillon to the draw. The TV was destroyed. The corporal was reduced in rank and transferred to a command that didn't require photographers to stand guard duty with a loaded .45 caliber pistol.

My grade school buddy, Sonny Bice, had transferred from Parris Island to the Marine Barracks at Fort Meade, Maryland, in September 1960. The Barracks was opened in 1953 and assigned to guard the National Security Agency there. The Marines were relieved of that duty and the Barracks closed in 1978. While there, Bice competed as a member of the boxing team at Quantico. Bice and I were reunited in March 1961 when the Quantico Marines met the Roanoke Police Athletic League boxers at Quantico's Larson Gym. Unfortunately, it was not one of Bice's better nights. The Marines won five of the seven bouts. But, Bice lost his fight on a split decision.

The 1961, Quantico track and field relays lived up to its billing. More than forty colleges and eight hundred athletes entered the fifth annual three-day event. My centerfold coverage of the meet summed it up, "14 Meet Records Smashed During Relays." Among the most memorable, Marine Lieutenant and Olympian Pete Close set a meet record in the 880 and ran the fastest mile of the year as of April 15. Penn State's Bob Brown set a meet record while winning the 100-yard dash. Olympian Bo Robertson, an Army lieutenant stationed at Fort Lee, Virginia, set a meet record in the broad jump. Olympian Rolando Cruz, competing independently, set a meet record in the pole vault at 14' 10".

In May, Quantico's Corporal John Uelses cleared 15' in the pole vault during the Penn State Relays. Two months later he vaulted 15' 4 1/2" to win the event in a meet between American and Russian athletes in Moscow. Cpl Uelses would add more height to his vaults in 1962. More on that later.

Summer 1961, my writing attracted the attention of Quantico's Special Services Officer, Lieutenant Colonel George McHenry, and he recommended I be meritoriously promoted to lance corporal. My commanding officer agreed. I would now be receiving ninety-nine dollars and thirty-seven cents a month.

Following promotion to lance corporal at Quantico in 1961.

The 1961 Christmas Basketball Tournament produced another

championship for the Quantico Marines, their seventh since the tournament began in 1954. Teams entered included Indiana State College, the Philadelphia Textile Institute, Catawba College, Acadia University from Canada, and St. Michael's of Vermont. Quantico defeated the Indiana State Teachers 75–66 in the final game.

Over the 1961 Christmas holidays, I was on leave and devoted several days to writing sports for the Norfolk *Ledger-Dispatch*. On December 27, a piece I did promoting an upcoming professional wrestling match was published. The following day, over a byline that read By Bob Bowen, Staff Correspondent, the headline read "The Spartans: Is It Their Year?" The story previewed an upcoming basketball tournament hosted by the Norfolk State Spartans.

My reporting on the tournament continued each day for the next three days, "Revenge Win Breaks Jinx in Tourney for Spartans," "Speed Holds Key for Norfolk State," and after the final game, "Teamwork Salvaged in Spartans' Loss."

The *Ledger-Dispatch* had a name change in 1962. It became the *Ledger-Star*. (The *Ledger-Star*, an evening newspaper, ceased publication in 1995, leaving Norfolk with only the morning newspaper, the *Virginian-Pilot*.)

On January 3, a *Ledger-Star* headline read: "Foul Shots Win for Tigers." My story was about a high school basketball game between the Oscar Smith Tigers and the Warwick Farmers. The Tigers won 57–44. My published report on January 4, read "A Sister's Prodding, Alumnus Send State Two College Stars." The story told about two student standouts at a Norfolk State College, Earl Hunter and Jimmy Johnson.

On January 10, I was back in Marine Corps uniform, but in Norfolk for a basketball game between Quantico and the Navy's Sublant Sea Raiders. The headline read "Enlisted Man 'Outranks' His Officers." The report described how Lance Corporal Roland Betts provided the needed rebound strength at both ends of the court, permitting the predominate officers on the Marine team to outscore the Navy, 87–66.

I celebrated my twenty-first birthday, January 12, by writing about a basketball game between Quantico and the Naval Air Station Flyers for the Quantico *Sentry*. That game was also in Norfolk. Coach Capt

Rottsalk was not happy with the way the Marines played, but they won by ten points, 90–80.

I left Quantico on January 19, 1962. I signed for travel orders that day to the Armed Forces Radio and Television Station on Okinawa. I had to be at Marine Barracks, Treasure Island in San Francisco by February 10, 1962, for further transportation to Okinawa. In the interim, I would be on leave.

CHAPTER 5

Between Assignments

*"I don't know whether war is an interlude during
peace, or peace is an interlude during war.*
~ George Clemenceau, French Statesman

The first thing on my leave schedule was a trip to Warwick, Rhode Island. A couple of college students from Salve Regina Women's College in Newport, Rhode Island, had driven to Quantico to cheer for the St. Michael's of Vermont basketball team during the annual Christmas tournament. One of the girls, Anne S. and I had hit it off. Her hairdo resembled Little Orphan Annie's red mop. I was invited to spend a weekend with her and her family before I left for Okinawa. Her father was a sitting judge and former state senator.

I took the bus from Quantico to Newport the evening of January 19, arriving the following morning. We had planned to go skiing that day. I had never been on skies before, but Anne assured me it would be fun so I agreed. As a young Marine, it would not be fitting to turn down the invitation.

Her brother was away at school. He and I were about the same size, so I wore his ski outfit. We drove from Warwick to Mount Snow, Vermont. It took about three and a half hours to complete the drive. Along the way, heavy snow began falling and the temperature dropped rapidly. We slid on the pavement when we turned into the ice-covered parking lot at the lodge, but managed to park without hitting anyone or anything. The ski lift had been closed because of the weather. The ski slopes were closed—thank God.

We had lunch in the lodge restaurant, turned around and drove back to Warwick. During the somewhat longer drive home, because of the weather, I continually lamented the fact we were not able to ski. Privately I was thanking my lucky stars.

I stayed in their home, and since there was no extra bedroom, I slept with Anne—with an eighteenth century bundling board firmly in place, dividing the bed in half. I had my side. She had her side—a far cry from bunk beds in the barracks.

My return trip to Norfolk was scheduled for Sunday evening. We awoke that morning and Anne invited me to attend early Mass at her Catholic church. I'm a Methodist. I had never attended a Catholic church. I told her I was uneasy about attending for the first time without knowing the procedure. "Don't worry," she said. "Just keep your eye on me and do what I do." Sounded like a piece of cake, so I agreed.

We entered the church, walked down the aisle, and when Anne reached her pew, she knelt to genuflect. I was following so closely that I fell over her. We made it through the rest of the service without any incidents, but I haven't been in a Catholic church since then unless it was to attend a funeral or a nondenominational service.

Brunch followed. It was as if Anne's family was going all out to make an impression on their guest. The table was set for a king. I've never seen so much silverware and sparkling glasses. I grew up with depression glasses and dishes found in boxes of cereal or laundry detergent. We seldom had enough knives, forks, or spoons to go around unless Mom was using her wedding silverware for some special occasion.

The main dish was Cornish hen. I had never eaten fowl fancier than chicken or turkey. I had no idea how to eat a Cornish hen, but I did know enough to slice a piece of chicken or turkey when the platter reached me and to pass it on to the person sitting next to me. So, when, as the guest, I was given the first Cornish hen, I cut off a leg and thigh and passed what was left to the person on my right. At least I passed it in the correct direction!

I don't remember anything else about that brunch, except feebly laughing off the "pass the Cornish hen gaff" and muddling my way through the rest of the meal. That afternoon, Anne gave me a driving tour of Newport. She drove past her college, housed in the 1892 mansion, Ochre Court, then down Ocean Drive, past the historic mansions, beaches, and rocky coves dotted with boulders and stones of every size and shape—all beaten smooth by the churning surf of Narraganset Bay. The drive ended with a view of Castle Hill Lighthouse. It was commissioned in 1874 to warn mariners sailing to Newport of the dangers of the Bay's east passage. The lighthouse was first built as a watchtower in 1740.

Anne and I exchanged several letters after I arrived on Okinawa, but nothing serious ever developed. After my stumbling performance at the church and total lack of etiquette during brunch, it was understandable that our friendship was on the wane before it ever got underway.

On February 2, 1962, I was sitting in my Mom's living room, watching news on her small black & white television. The sports announcer led off his segment with a report on Cpl Uelses clearing 16' in the pole vault that night at the Millrose Games in New York City's Madison Square Garden. Cpl Uelses, stationed at Quantico, was the first man to vault that high.

I called *Ledger-Star* Editor Turner Dozier at his home and asked if he would like a special report on Cpl Uelses' record vault. There was no hesitation. The answer was, "Yes." My R. C. Allen typewriter was still in my old bedroom. I used it to prepare my report on the first man—a Marine—to clear 16' in the pole vault.

The double-deck headline spread across a full page in the February 3, Saturday sports section. It read, "Super-Vaulter Conquers His Fear of Height. 16-Foot Flight Tops in History." It was bylined "By Lance Cpl. Bob Bowen" and described as a "*Ledger-Star* Special."

When I turned in my story Saturday morning, I asked about doing a follow-up story on Cpl Uelses. He was born in Germany. I said his story would be interesting. Dozier agreed. So, the following day, I traveled by bus to Quantico to interview Cpl Uelses, arrange for some photos, and return home to write my feature.

The follow-up report turned into a two-part series. The first story appeared February 7. It was headlined "I'll Get Rubber Pole—Uelses." The Marine had used a fiberglass pole for his 16' vault and there had been questions and concerns raised about using fiberglass for the competition. Cpl Uelses' response was that if the fiberglass pole were banned, he'd have one made of rubber.

The second part of the two-part series was headlined "German Vaults From Hitler Camp to Track Heights." It went on to describe Cpl Uelses' life as a youth under Hitler, his move to Miami to live with an aunt, his high school athletic endeavors, and his time in the Marine Corps.

CHAPTER 6

Okinawa Bound

Go West, Young Man.
~ Horace Greeley

If you go far enough west, you'll reach the Far East. Go figure.

I traveled by train from Norfolk to San Francisco, California, arriving on February 10. My flight to Okinawa was scheduled for February 24. I had two weeks with nothing to do but routine chores at Treasure Island, an occasional walk around the island to see what remained of buildings and other structures left there from the 1939 Golden Gate International Exposition, and to go on sightseeing excursions into San Francisco.

On one trip into San Francisco one evening, I wandered into a bar to rest and enjoy a beer. Having recently turned twenty-one, I could now buy a beer at any pub. I was in uniform. I asked the bartender for a Budweiser and he asked for my identification. I proudly displayed my military ID card showing my date of birth as January 12, 1941, twenty-one years and one month earlier. He winked, a sign that my youth would be our secret, and popped the top on a Bud. "Glass?" he asked. "No, this is fine," I replied.

It wasn't long before the night's main attraction was announced—a twist contest. The dance had taken the country by storm. The first recording of the song, "The Twist," was released in 1959 by Hank Ballard and the Midnighters. It was later released by Chubby Checker. It hit the top of the Billboard Top 100 songs in September 1960. It was back on top in January 1962.

I learned to do the Texas Bop one summer in North Carolina. My cousin, Patrick Hannifin, and I frequently traveled to Mooresville in the summer of 1955. A natural gas pipeline was being constructed from Texas to points north, and the pipeline workers had brought their families with them. Pat and I made the thirty-mile trip, often by hitchhiking, to see the daughters. They taught us the Texas Bop. Seven years later, it was easily converted to the Twist.

When the dance contest was announced that night in the San Francisco bar, I glanced around the room and my eyes fell on two girls sitting by themselves at a table. I walked over, introduced myself, and learned that they were students at the University of Maryland. They had taken some time off from their studies to visit San Francisco. Marilyn, one of the college students, accepted my offer to enter the contest. As Gomer Pyle would have said, "Surprise. Surprise!" We won the contest and split the two dollar top prize.

I traveled on a Marine Corps bus to Travis Air Force Base near Fairfield, California, on February 24 for the flight to Okinawa. The Military Air Transport C-118 Liftmaster (Douglas DC-6 equivalent) made stops at Hawaii, Wake, Guam, and Japan before arriving on Okinawa. I thought we'd never get there. The flight to the Far East took about forty hours, including ground time. My orders show I arrived at 9:20 p.m., February 26. I reported to Camp Smedley D. Butler and was assigned to the Armed Forces Radio and Television Station.

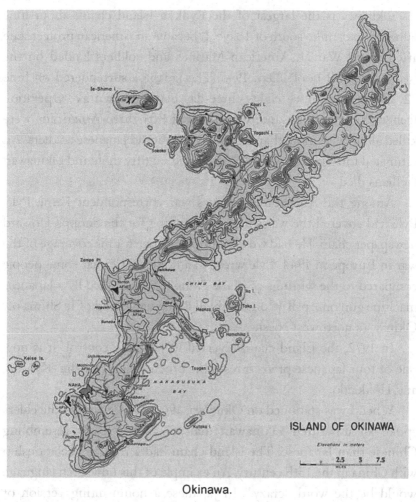

Okinawa.

AFRTS, Okinawa.

Okinawa is the largest of the Ryukyu Island chain, about nine hundred sixty miles south of Tokyo. It became an American protectorate after World War II. American Marines and soldiers landed on the island on April Fool's Day, 1945. The Japanese surrendered on June 22. During the fierce eighty-three-day battle, known as "Operation Iceberg," twelve thousand, one hundred fifty-three Americans were killed along with more than ninety-five thousand Japanese soldiers. An estimated forty-two thousand to one hundred fifty thousand Okinawan civilians died.

Among the American dead was war correspondent Ernie Pyle. Pyle had covered the war since its beginning for the Scripps-Howard newspaper chain. He had won the Pulitzer Prize for his coverage of the war in Europe in 1944. Pyle wrote in a homey style that some people compared to the writings of Mark Twain. He was killed by a Japanese machine gun on April 18 on the small Ryukyuan island of Ie Shima off Okinawa's northwest coast.

In 1972, the island chain reverted to Japanese control. It is now one of four Japanese prefectures—the others being Honshu, Kyushu, and Hokkaido.

When I was stationed on Okinawa, 1962–1964, many of the elders spoke an unwritten Okinawan dialect—more closely resembling Chinese than Japanese. The island chain had a tributary relationship with China in the 15th century. An example of this unwritten language would be the word "crazy." In Japanese a noninsulting version of "crazy" is "bakadanaa." The Okinawan word for "crazy" is "frog-wah." Bear in mind my spelling has no foundation other than the sound. The Okinawan language was not written.

Joe Takamiyagi, the station's "jack of all trades," liked to tell the story about an internment camp set up for Okinawan civilians after the war. One day, an MP approached an old man tending his potato patch at the edge of the compound. Thinking the MP was going to confiscate his potatoes, the old man stood up, crossed his arms in front of his chest, and said "What time! What time!" a phonetic spelling of the Okinawan words for "it's mine." Hearing the English "What time," the MP glanced at his watch and said "nine thirty," which was

Okinawan for "take all you want." The old man smiled and said "knee-hey-debbie-doe," Okinawan for "thank you." The MP walked away scratching his head.

The temperature on Okinawa seldom drops below 68 degrees, making it ideal for water sports. I spent much of my free time snorkeling. The ocean surrounding the island is clear and abounding with colorful fish of all sizes. The color of the coral formations takes your breath away. Many of Okinawa's beaches are covered with dead coral, but the coral is often teaming with living sea urchins. Their sharp spines can be very painful. Two other concerns for the swimmer are the Moray eels and poisonous sea snakes. The wise snorkeler on Okinawa never enters the water without a knife and a spear gun.

Mating pair of poisonous Habu snakes.

On land, a major concern is the Habu, a venomous pit viper, found throughout the island. The small Asian mongoose was introduced on Okinawa in the early 1900s to help control the snakes.

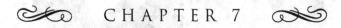

CHAPTER 7

AFRTS

*Television is an invention that permits you to be
entertained in your living room by people
you wouldn't have in your home.*

~ David Frost

Single members of the military assigned to the Armed Forces Radio and Television Station lived in Building 107 on Kadena Air Base. We were assigned two to a room. My roommate was Jimmy Carter, a lance corporal from California. He spent all of his extra money on suits and shirts he had made in town. He planned on being the best-dressed man in Los Angeles when he was discharged after his tour on Okinawa.

Most of us living in the barracks ate at the Kadena bowling alley. It was within walking distance and prices were reasonable, just what a young enlisted man with limited funds needed. My favorite was omurice, a fried rice concoction containing tiny pieces of pork, beef, shrimp, or chicken and green onions—mounded on a plate and served covered with a thin egg omelet. It was delicious with catsup added. Once a week, the enlisted club served lobster tails for fifty cents apiece.

Haircuts were fifty cents at the Paris barbershop in town on Gate Two Street. Mud packs and shaves were also fifty cents each, as was a face, head, and back massage. For two dollars, I could spend two hours relaxing in the barber's chair. I did this often.

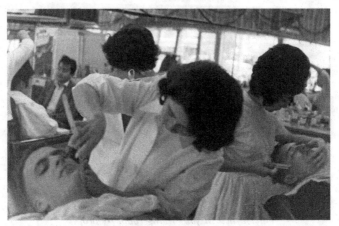

Weekly haircut . . . Paris barbershop, Gate Two Street.

Other Marine broadcasters in the AFRTS newsroom at one time or another during my time there were Staff Sergeants Joe Pratt, Bert Presson, and Bill Rich; Sergeants Frank Beardsley, Al Benn, George Brown, Tom Kraak, Bill May, Bobby McKinley, Ron Mingus, and Ken Warrior; Corporals Mike Grove, Jerry Shelton, Paul Thompson, and Bob Wright; Lance Corporals Jimmie Carter and Willie Gartner; and Privates First Class Marty Schoen and Carl White. The only non-Marines in the newsroom were Navy Seamen Jerry "Brownie" Brown and Joe Nemichek. Seaman Brown was from Louisville, Kentucky. He was my primary snorkeling partner.

Typhoons, the Pacific Ocean version of a hurricane, lash out throughout the year, often targeting Okinawa. My first experience with a typhoon was in April 1962. I had been on the island for less than two months when warnings went out for Typhoon Georgia. It brought high winds to Okinawa, but never unleashed its full force on the island. It eventually dwindled to a breeze as it went across Japan's eastern coast.

Marine staff, AFRTS Okinawa, 1963.
Front Row (l-r): Sgt Bobby McKinley, Sgt Frank Beardsley,
Sgt Bert Presson, CWO Bill Driscoll, Sgt George Brown, Sgt Bill May.
Back Row (l-r): Cpl Paul Thompson, LCpl Willie Gartner, LCpl Jimmy Carter,
Sgt Al Benn, Cpl Jerry Shelton, LCpl Bob Bowen.

Typhoon Hope was declared a 100-mile-per-hour Category 2 typhoon on May 20. It's eye was south of Okinawa. With conditions this severe, all of the unaccompanied men assigned to AFRTS had to report to the studio at Rycom Plaza in the center of the island. There, we would broadcast constant updates on the storm's location and provide around-the-clock entertainment by televising one movie after another.

AFRTS was staffed by broadcasters from all four services. Under typhoon conditions we gathered at the station and uncrated the folding canvas cots we kept there, along with the C-rations. Those of us in the newsroom would take turns driving around the island when conditions were not too severe. We'd take Polaroid photos of the empty streets and any damage caused by the storm and televise them so troops who could not go outside could see the current conditions. On occasion, we'd find an Okinawan store open and buy some fresh fruit or other items to supplement the C-rats.

AFRTS microphone.

The "all-clear" sounded for Typhoon Hope on May 21. That didn't end the 1962 typhoon season. It would continue through November 27. Okinawa was not seriously threatened at any time in 1962 despite thirty storms reaching a strength sufficient to be given a name. Most of them passed north or south of the island.

There were twenty-five named storms in the Pacific in 1963, nineteen of them reaching typhoon status. In 1964, there were thirty-nine named storms making it the most active Pacific storm season in recorded history, at that time—twenty-five of them elevated to typhoons, and seven of them classified as super typhoons, with winds of at least one hundred fifty miles an hour.

Bill Murray, coach of the Duke University Blue Devils football team, toured the Far East in the summer of 1962. He conducted football clinics for the military in Hawaii, Korea, and Okinawa. My report on his visit to Okinawa appeared in the Norfolk *Ledger-Star* in August. The three-column headline read, "Blue Devil Coach Foresees Good Year." It was bylined "By Lance Cpl. Bob Bowen, *Ledger-Star* Correspondent."

For most of my time on "The Rock," as Marines call Okinawa, I wrote and announced a daily sports program for both radio and television. At the onset of the college and professional football season, I wrote pre-season "specials" complete with predictions of how each season might unfold. I was seldom correct, but how often can any sportscaster make a claim of perfection. The troops enjoyed the programs. They fulfilled a primary goal of AFRTS "to inform, educate and entertain."

Daily television sports show.

I also prepared a weekly "This is Okinawa" television news show and hosted a weekly game show called Hodge-Podge-Lodge. The game show was carried "live" and involved viewers calling in to unscramble a series of letters to correctly spell a word. Don't remember if correct answers were rewarded beyond the caller being recognized by name as someone with a streak of brilliance.

"This is Okinawa" radio program, 1962.

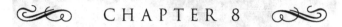

CHAPTER 8

Bob Hope Arrives

I have seen what a laugh can do.
It can transform almost unbearable tears
into something bearable, even hopeful.

~ Bob Hope

In December 1962, I was assigned to go to Kadena Air Base to meet and interview Bob Hope and members of his USO Christmas Show. He arrived the day after Christmas. Two performances were scheduled for Okinawa. I interviewed the popular entertainer shortly after he stepped off the C-130 cargo plane transporting him and his troupe. Staff Sergeant Bert Presson, the senior enlisted Marine at AFRTS, was there making photographs. When the arrival interviews were over, we rushed back to the station.

While I was preparing my report, complete with segments of the taped interview, SSgt Presson was in the darkroom processing the film and making prints to be televised to illustrate my report. Army Staff Sergeant Jay Lehman was the duty announcer. He presented my report in his usual highly professional manner. I still have the three-inch audio tape reel containing my interview of Bob Hope, and a seven-inch audio tape reel of his performance.

Others traveling with Bob Hope in 1962 included Lana Turner, Janis Paige, Anita Bryant, Jerry Colonna, Peter Leeds, Les Brown and his Band of Renown, and Amedee Chabot, recently crowned Miss USA during a beauty pageant in Huntington, West Virginia, the city of my birth.

Interviewing Bob Hope following his arrival on Okinawa
for his USO Christmas show, December 1962,
From l-r: Janis Paige, Anita Bryant,
LCpl Robert "Bob" Bowen, Bob Hope.

I worked the late shift at the station on December 27, so I couldn't attend Bob Hope's evening show at Fort Buckner, but when the curtain raised on his show that afternoon, I was in the front row with camera in hand. Photos I made during the performance have provided many memories over the past fifty-five years.

Bob Hope and Lana Turner, 1962 Christmas Show, Okinawa.

Okinawa was a thirteen-month assignment for Marines in the early 1960s. At the end of 1962, with my tour coming to an end, I requested an extension of my assignment. It was approved on January 14, 1963. This gave me another year of snorkeling, dodging typhoons, and learning the skills of a radio and television broadcaster. Life was good.

Seaman Brown and Sgt Beardsley were my snorkeling partners. And, having been on Okinawa for a year before I arrived, they were my underwater instructors.

We seldom missed an opportunity to explore the water surrounding the island, either the East China Sea to the west or the Philippine Sea to the east. Both were brilliantly clear, teaming with every imaginable kind of fish, poisonous sea snakes, moray eels, multicolored coral, and sea urchins.

Snorkeling on Okinawa, 1962.

World War II had ended less than twenty years earlier and Okinawa was the scene of some of the bitterest fighting of the Pacific Campaign.

The island still bore the scars of that war and when we searched for new beaches to explore we often found remnants of the fighting. On one such occasion near Kadena Air Base, I found a rusty tin can in a cave at the end of an inlet leading from the East China Sea. In it, was part of an old Japanese military map, probably belonging to the Japanese soldiers who occupied the cave during the war. I gave the map to the Army Museum at Fort Buckner.

Back in my day, there were basically two ways for an enlisted man to get promoted in the Marine Corps. Meritorious promotions were advancements in rank based on outstanding performance in your current rank at a level that a person of the next higher rank was expected to demonstrate. I had received meritorious promotions to private first class and lance corporal.

Being promoted to corporal, the junior noncommissioned officer rank, required compiling a score high enough to make a specific grade established for your occupational field. This "cutting score," as it was called, was based on your latest physical fitness test score, your latest rifle marksmanship score, your average daily performance rating, average conduct score, time-in-grade at your current rank, and any self-education.

I don't recall what the cutting score was for the corporal's promotion cycle in 1963, nor the score required for promotion in my occupational specialty, but I made it. I was promoted to corporal on January 1, 1963. I would be earning one hundred forty-five dollars a month. In April 1963, I extended my tour again. I was now scheduled to leave Okinawa in June 1964.

In May 1963, I went to Camp Butler to cover a change of command ceremony at the Third Marine Division. Major General James M. Masters was assuming command. For a brief time, his younger brother, Brigadier General John H. Masters, would be the assistant division commander. In his acceptance speech, MajGen Masters told the assembled Marines, "I'm sure you've heard that you cannot serve two masters. Well, now, you will have to." The two-Masters command lasted only a few days. BGen Masters was then transferred to Headquarters Marine Corps in Washington, D.C., where he was assigned as the assistant quartermaster general.

In June 1963, a United Artist motion picture camera crew arrived to film the SU-19 Albatross seaplane. The movie, "Flight from Ashiya," about an Air Force Rescue Service located in Japan, was being filmed for release in 1964. It starred Yul Brynner, Richard Widmark, and George Chakaris.

The author filming scenes being filmed by Hollywood cameramen on location for "Flight from Ashiya," starring Yul Brenner, off Okinawa, 1963.

The motion picture film crew came to Okinawa to shoot some scenes of the orange and gray seaplanes landing and taking off from the ocean to use in "Flight from Ashiya." The ocean off White Beach on Okinawa's southeast coast, was chosen for the repeated "touch and go" scenes. Two seaplanes were used. The Hollywood filmmakers had photographers on each plane. I was on one of them with a Bell & Howell motion picture camera. My coverage of the filming was shared with AFRTS viewers that night.

CHAPTER 9

Career Decision

In any moment of decision, the best thing you can do is the right thing, the next best thing is the wrong thing, and the worst thing you can do is nothing.
~ Theodore Roosevelt, 26th President of the United States

In early July, I received a letter from Mom. My sister, Dolores, was getting married—to a sailor. I had left home eighteen months earlier and my sister wasn't even dating. Now she was getting married. I'd never met the man. This required investigation.

I explained my problem to my first sergeant at Camp Butler. His solution was for me to reenlist one year early and use my reenlistment bonus to finance a leave home so I could check on my sister's seafaring suitor. The only problem was I'd have to reenlist for six years to get a bonus large enough to pay for the round-trip airfare to Norfolk from the west coast. After thinking it over I decided it was the only thing to do.

Adding another six years to the three I was about to complete would give me nine years of Marine Corps service when 1969 rolled around. Why not? I was healthy. I was only 22. I was single. Above all, I enjoyed my job and was doing what I wanted to do. So, at 11:15 a.m. July 31, 1963, I raised my right hand, took the oath for another six years, picked up my reenlistment bonus and leave papers, arranged for a space-available flight to Travis Air Force Base, and flew to California.

Before reenlisting, I received my first Good Conduct Medal, an award earned by Marines every three years if their conduct had been at a sufficient high level throughout the three-year period covered. In my case, the three years began when I enlisted in the Marine Corps and ended July 28, 1963. So, when I left on reenlistment leave I had a Good Conduct ribbon and my rifle expert and pistol marksman badges displayed above my left dress shirt pocket. I felt like an "old timer." When I arrived in California, I purchased a round trip ticket from San Francisco to Norfolk, boarded my plane and settled down for the long cross-country flight. I took a cab from the Norfolk Municipal Airport to Mom's home in Norview, a five-mile drive.

I met my sister's sailor. He appeared to be okay, so I gave my blessings to the marriage (not that it was needed nor requested) and devoted the rest of my leave to visiting with old friends at my church, and with the writers in the *Ledger-Star* sports department.

I had to be back on Okinawa by August 30, so I flew back to San Francisco on August 25. After arriving there, I took a bus to Travis Air Force Base and signed up for a space-available flight back to Okinawa. The first available flight was for Hickam Air Force Base in Hawaii. My orders did not permit travel to Hawaii, only between Okinawa and CONUS, the Continental United States. So, I had to get my orders modified to permit me to visit our 50th island state.

When I checked in at the Marine desk at Travis Air Force Base, I discovered that I had misplaced my shot card. Without a record of my immunizations, I could not fly to Okinawa. This meant a whole battery of shots in one day—tetanus, diphtheria, typhoid, cholera, and hepatitis were mandatory, as well as polio, but polio was an oral vaccine. So, I went to the Corpsman on duty and he decided to fix me up. He asked if I minded getting everything at the same time. Not knowing any better, I said "Okay."

The Corpsman proceeded to load every required immunization into one syringe. One shot would be better than five, I reasoned, but when the thick mixture began ripping its way through the muscle of my left shoulder I almost fainted. I don't know if the Corpsman was being cute or really wanted to prevent me from having to endure five separate shots, but it took several hours for the knot of medicine to spread through my body, and it hurt far worse than five separate shots would have. There were no lasting ill effects, but I've been leery of needles—and Corpsmen—ever since that experience.

During the layover in Honolulu, I took a cab to Waikiki Beach. At one of the many hotels lining the beach, I listened to a performance by singer Don Ho and rubbed elbows at the bar with Peter Yarrow of the Peter, Paul and Mary singing trio. The next day, I took a cab to the Punchbowl, the National Memorial Cemetery of the Pacific—final resting place for some of the American servicemen killed in the Pacific during World War I, World War II, and Korea.

Today, the cemetery also contains the bodies of many of those killed in Vietnam. More than fifty-three thousand veterans and their dependents are buried there.

I caught a flight for Okinawa two days later and arrived there the morning of August 30—thirteen hours before my thirty days reenlistment leave expired. The following week I received a large envelope from Mom. She had found my shot card after I left home. "I thought you might need this," she said.

I was now committed for nine years in the Marine Corps, eleven years shy of a full twenty-year career, but I had already decided I was a "career Marine." My sister's marriage ended in divorce. But, my reenlistment and trip home to meet her sailor was fortuitous for me.

When I arrived on Okinawa in 1962, Marine First Lieutenant Richard A. "Dick" Trafas was the Assistant Officer in Charge of AFRTS. 1stLt Trafas was an outstanding football player at St. Thomas, a private Catholic school in Minnesota. In 1957, he was drafted as an offensive end by the Detroit Lions professional football team. That was the same year the Lions drafted a quarterback from Occidental College in Los Angeles, Jack Kemp. Neither 1stLt Trafas nor Kemp made the final cut. Kemp joined the Army Reserves and later made a name for himself by leading the Buffalo Bills to two championships in the AFL before entering politics. He was named to the Greater Buffalo Sports Hall of Fame in 1992. 1stLt Trafas received a commission in the Marine Corps. He was inducted into the St. Thomas Athletic Hall of Fame in 2007.

The entire AFRTS Okinawa staff in late 1962 during the transition of 1stLt Dick Trafas and CWO Bill Driscoll as Assistant Officer in Charge. Front Row (l-r): 1stLt Trafas, Major William Tapie, CWO Bill Driscoll.

1stLt Trafas left Okinawa in 1963. He was replaced by Marine Chief Warrant Officer Bill Driscoll. The senior officers in charge of the broadcast facility during my time there were either Air Force Majors William L. Tapie, or Damon E. Eckles. Maj Tapie was there when I arrived, Maj Eckles when I left.

CHAPTER 10

A Torch is Passed

Life is no brief candle to me. It is a sort of splendid
torch which I have got a hold of for the moment,
and I want to make it burn as brightly as possible
before handing it onto future generations.
~ George Bernard Shaw

CWO Driscoll was a stickler for physical fitness and seemed to enjoy taking "his" AFRTS Marines on long marches every month. He was an ardent believer in the philosophy that every Marine was a rifleman regardless of his MOS. And, Marines marched everywhere. We were scheduled for such a march the morning of November 23, 1963.

We were up by 4 a.m.—getting dressed, checking our packs, M-14 rifles, and other gear, preparing to go to the station to begin our march. Allowing for a thirteen-hour time difference, it was 3 p.m. Friday afternoon in Dallas, Texas. Two and one-half hours earlier—while we were sleeping—a sniper opened fire on the presidential motorcade in downtown Dallas. At 1:00 p.m., Dallas time, President John F. Kennedy was pronounced dead. This all took place while we were sleeping.

CWO Driscoll arrived at our barracks on Kadena Air Base at about 4:30 a.m. The quiet of the morning was broken when he slammed the door open. He called us all together and briefed us as best he could with the limited information he had. He then ordered us to drop our packs and get to the station. "Some son of a bitch shot our president," he said. "We have a job to do. The troops need to be informed." Sgt Beardsley was the senior man in the newsroom. His instructions were brief and to the point. "You heard the Gunner," he said. "Drop your gear. Secure your weapon. Get to the station. We have work to do."

The Air Force had assigned a truck for AFRTS to use to transport troops between the barracks and the station. We also used it to get around the island to cover events. That morning, everyone piled onboard and we rushed to the station.

By the time we arrived, Sgt Beardsley had developed a plan. The events in Dallas were particularly painful for him. He was a proud Texan. Vice President Lyndon Baines Johnson was a Texan. The assassin, soon to be identified as Lee Harvey Oswald, was a former Marine who defected to Moscow, married, and recently returned home and settled in the Dallas/Fort Worth area.

Sgt Frank Beardsley, news director,
led the Kennedy assassination coverage.

Sgt Beardsley would produce our special report on the assassination.

He assigned one man to write the television news story. One man had the task of writing the news for our radio audience. Another man would write the "world reaction" story—what the leaders of other countries were saying about the assassination. One man was assigned to cull all recent news magazines for photos of the president. These were clipped, attached to flip boards, and used to illustrate the television report. A small Dage television camera was used for the flip board.

Cpl Jerry Shelton (l) was assigned to write our special television report on the Assassination of President Kennedy. It was my (r) job to keep the AP and UPI teletype machines cleared so Cpl Shelton would have a constant supply of fresh source material for his report.

Sgt Beardsley sent one Marine to the library at Kadena Air Base to check out books on President Kennedy. While there, he searched the shelves for books about the assassinations of Presidents Lincoln, Garfield, and McKinley. That information was woven into the fabric of our report of President Kennedy's assassination. Another man searched through the AP and UPI film clips we had on file for footage of the president. These, too, were used to tell about President Kennedy's life and illustrate our report of his death.

I had the task of monitoring our teletype machines. We subscribed to the AP and UPI teletype news services. Both machines were working overtime churning out the news. The bells announcing arriving bulletins rang out frequently. It was a challenge to make sure neither machine ran out of paper and that the inked ribbons were producing copy that could be read. Kennedy stories were kept separate from the other news coming over the teletype machines. I took these to the Marines assigned to report on other news events.

Throughout the day, our listeners received regular updates on the situation back home. Vice President Johnson was traveling with President Kennedy. At 2:00 p.m., one hour after he was declared dead at Parkland Hospital, a casket containing the body of the 35th president was placed on Air Force One. Vice President Johnson was on the plane. Thirty-eight minutes into the flight, with his wife, Lady Bird, on his right and First Lady, Jacqueline Kennedy, on his left, Johnson took the oath of office. He was now the 36th President of the United States.

The AFRTS audience received almost constant news that day. There were occasional bulletins, such as when Johnson became our President. Our lengthy television report aired that night at 6 p.m. and again—with updates—at 10:00 p.m. Our radio audience received hourly and half-hourly updates throughout the day. We took our job seriously at AFRTS. That day, we held back tears as we went about our job of reporting the news and were especially proud of our product.

An old friend from the Norview Methodist Church, Worth "Woody" Norman joined the Marine Corps and was assigned duty as a bandsman. On December 24, 1963, he arrived in Naha, Okinawa onboard the USS *General W. A. Mann* (AP-112) troopship. Some fifty years later, Norman told me that as the ship approached Naha its loud speakers were broadcasting the news from the local Armed Forces Radio and Television station. He said, "I heard you on AFRTS announcing our imminent arrival. It was so good to hear your familiar, hometown (Norfolk, VA) voice."

Three years later, after Norman and I had returned to the States, Norman was with the band at Quantico when he met and fell in

My Life and Lens

love with Patricia Ann Padrick. I provided the photographic coverage of their wedding. Norman, an Anglican Deacon, and his Patricia celebrated their fiftieth wedding anniversary in 2016.

My first wedding assignment, April 8, 1966.
Woody Norman and Patricia Ann Padrick.

In January 1963, I received orders assigning me the additional MOS of 4313, Radio and Television Information Man. The MOS 4312, Press Information Man, remained my primary military occupational specialty.

In March, 1964, I was named AFRTS Man of the Month and assigned as chief announcer of the TV section. My job included scheduling all of the announcers for on-air work and coordinating the schedule with the TV staff director. On March 12, the English language. *Morning Star* newspaper published a story and photo about a new weekly television show being produced and directed by the AFRTS staff. The hour long program was "Tee-Vee Teahouse." It catered to the American wives on the island. Its' theme was "Where West Meets East." I was the audio director.

The Harlem Globetrotters came to Okinawa that month. Two performances were held at Stilwell Fieldhouse—March 20–21. Owner and founder, Abe Saperstein, Meadowlark Lemon, and two other members of the team, came to the AFRTS television studio on March 19. As the chief television announcer, I interviewed Saperstein and goofed around on the set with Lemon, the "Clown Prince," and the other players. The show received good reviews and helped ensure sold-out audiences at each of their performances the next two days.

An interview with Abe Saperstein, owner and founder of the Harlem Globetrotters.

In April 1964, I received another extension of my tour on Okinawa. "Barring unforeseen circumstances" as the extensions were always worded, my tour was extended until August 1965.

In July 1964, *Leatherneck* Magazine correspondent Staff Sergeant

Paul Berger arrived on Okinawa to gather material for a story about the AFRTS Marines. With camera in hand, he accompanied us on one of our marches, observed our daily routine at the station, visited our barracks at Kadena Air Base, and conducted one-on-one interviews.

Sgt Beardsley and I spoke to SSgt Berger while he was there. He had mentioned that the magazine would be looking for several writers later that year. Sgt Beardsley was expecting orders to leave Okinawa later that year and Sgt Berger said he would recommend that SSgt Beardsley be assigned to *Leatherneck* Magazine. SSgt Berger suggested I write a letter requesting my extension be canceled and that I be transferred to *Leatherneck* Magazine as well. He said he would do what he could for me on the other end. It was time to invoke the "barring unforeseen circumstances" clause attached to my latest extension.

On August 5, CWO Driscoll, SSgt Rich, and Sgt Beardsley traveled to Vietnam to gather material for a special report on Okinawa Marines and soldiers serving as advisors in South Vietnam. That ten-day visit produced a one-hour television feature titled "In Our Own Backyard." CWO Driscoll wrote the program. SSgt Rich was the principle cameraman. Sgt Beardsley produced and directed the show. When the special aired, I was in the TV announcer's booth, raising and lowering the volume on background music on cue. The program received high praise from throughout the island.

CHAPTER 11

1964 Olympics

Don't put a limit on anything. The more you dream, the further you get.
~ Michael Phelps,
Winner of a Record 23 Olympic Gold Medals

In 1959, Tokyo was chosen as the site of the 1964 Summer Olympics. During the two-week period preceding the opening ceremonies on October 10, I wrote, produced, and gave our television viewers a daily five-minute history of the Olympics, titled "Olympic Digest."

Olympic Digest.

When the games began, I scheduled myself for all of our television coverage of the international competition. Our sister military broadcast facility on the Japanese mainland, the Far East Network, had an agreement with NHK, the Japanese commercial television network. A simulcast schedule was devised. When desirable, NHK would use the FEN English language audio description of the Olympics and FEN would use the live video coverage broadcast by NHK. We also received this broadcast feed on Okinawa.

As the saying goes "the best made plans of mice and men" do not always go as planned. Several times during the agreed upon simulcast schedule, NHK switched in midstream to some event in which a Japanese athlete or team was excelling. This was perfectly understandable. We see that all the time with coverage of international events here in the States. When this happened during the Tokyo Olympic, I was often stuck in the AFRTS television announcer's booth without a clue about how to describe what was going on.

We could not broadcast the Japanese language description of the events. The American announcers at FEN were continuing to maintain their schedule, but we were not seeing images of those events. The only thing for me to do was turn off the audio, turn on my microphone, and try to present a sensible play-by-play of the ping pong match or judo competition that suddenly appeared on the screen. An Okinawan engineer was helpful when it came to identifying the athletes.

At one point during a particularly long nonscheduled period of televised judo, one of the Army officers living near AFRTS rushed to the station with a book describing judo rules and techniques. It was greatly appreciated, but by the time I searched and found a particular technique being used, the men of the "gentle way" sport would be engaged in an entirely different technique.

Again, our television audience appreciated our efforts. Some of them actually thought I was at the Games providing "live" coverage. Shortly after the Olympics ended on October 24, the officer in charge of AFRTS, Major Eckels, sent a letter to my Marine Corps commanding officer at Camp Butler, commending me for my work on our Olympics coverage. The commanding officer used the letter as the basis for a

Meritorious Mast (written recognition of good work, higher than a letter of appreciation or letter of commendation). The Mast, dated December 2, 1964, read in part.

> *During the entire period of the 1964 Olympic telecasts there were many times when the simulcast schedule from FEN did not coincide with the picture, and we were left with the video portion and only Japanese language audio descriptions of the activities. To alleviate these periods, Sergeant Bowen worked with an interpreter to determine the names of the participating athletes, and then created an on-the-spot narration of the video action.*

> *Also, during the weeks preceding the Olympic Games, he wrote and produced a series of TV programs, "Olympic Digest." Through his diligent research and skill in presentation, these programs were most valuable entertainment for the sports minded people on Okinawa.*

> *Sergeant Bowen's efforts, initiative and skill in participating in these areas of radio and television coverage of the 1964 Olympic Games were commendable contributions to the public enjoyment of the games, and to the general morale of American military personnel and their dependents stationed on Okinawa.*

Sgt Beardsley's assignment to *Leatherneck* Magazine came through without a hitch. He was to leave AFRTS in December and report to the magazine in January. My request for a transfer took a little longer to arrange, but occurred quickly. I wrote a letter to Editor-Publisher Colonel Donald L. Dickson describing my background and accomplishments during my four-year career.

My letter must have impressed the colonel because on November 17, I received notification that my request for transfer to *Leatherneck* Magazine had been approved. At about the same time, my name appeared on the promotion list for sergeant. The promotion was effective December 1. So, a process that began with Cpl Bowen requesting a transfer ended with Sgt Bowen receiving final orders on December 12, directing me to report for duty at Headquarters Battalion, Headquarters Marine Corps at Henderson Hall in Arlington, Virginia. I checked in on December 22 and was further assigned to Company A for duty with *Leatherneck* Magazine.

I had arrived! A career that began four years earlier as a publicist and sports writer for a Marine Corps base newspaper; enhanced with experience as a writer, editor, and announcer with a radio and television station; had now been elevated to writing for the "Magazine of Marines," *Leatherneck* Magazine.

I left the States as a single twenty-one-year-old. I returned home as a married twenty-three-year-old. During my last year on Okinawa I married Katsuko "Katie" Iraha. Our first child, Jack, was born two months after returning to the states, on February 22, 1965, George Washington's birthday.

CHAPTER 12

Leatherneck, *the Magazine of Marines*

Ideally, the writer needs no audience other
than the few who understand.
It is immodest and greedy to want more.
~ Gore Vidal, Writer

Leatherneck Magazine offices were located on the second floor of Building 4, an old wooden building at Henderson Hall, across Southgate Road from the Navy Annex, next to the Army's Fort Myer. We parked behind the building on the side of a road that ran along Arlington National Cemetery. Henderson Hall was built in 1944. It was where the records of Marines assigned to Headquarters Marine Corps were kept. Headquarters. Marine Corps was in the Navy Annex, a huge complex originally built as a government warehouse.

Henderson Hall logo.

The Navy Annex is no more today. It was demolished in early 2013 to make room for more Arlington National Cemetery grave sites. HQMC offices are now located, for the most part, at either the Pentagon or the Marine Corp Base at Quantico, Virginia, about thirty miles south of the Pentagon. *Leatherneck* Magazine relocated to Quantico in 1972.

My first day at the magazine was devoted to meeting Editor-Publisher Colonel Don Dickson. The civilian staff members were called in and introduced one at a time: Managing Editor Karl Schuon, Copy Editor Ronnie Lyons, Photo Director Lou Lowery, and Art Director Bob Davis. Later that day, I was introduced to the Marine writers, photographers, and artists who were not on the road gathering new stories for the magazine.

When I turned in my orders at the magazine's administrative office, I was handed a copy of the latest Company Bulletin. At the top of the bulletin, someone in the admin office had penciled "WELCOME ABOARD!!!" At the bottom of the first column, I found my name. I had been assigned as Company A Duty NCO for January 31st.

During the seven years I was either assigned to or associated with *Leatherneck* Magazine I worked with some of the most talented and often goofy writers, photographers, artists, and officers I've ever known: Col Don Dickson, Col John Kleinhans, Maj King "Tiny" Thatenhurst, Capt Jerry Kershner, 1stLt Paul Glassburner, CWO_Bill Parker, Sgt Darla Anderberg, SSgt Tom Bartlett, Sgt Frank Beardsley, SSgt Paul Berger, Sgt Hank Berkowitz, Sgt George Broadley, Sgt Bob Burgoyne, Sgt Maggie Chavez, MSgt JoAnne Davis, MSgt Bud Devere, Sgt Dale "Daddy" Dye, SSgt Jim Elliott, GySgt Chris Evans, GySgt Ed Evans, GySgt Bill Ferris, MSgt Herb Freeman, Cpl Tom Gettings, Cpl Jimmy Giles, Sgt Bill Gnatzig, and SSgt Rich Groscost

Also, SSgt Harvey Hall, Cpl Stosh Hallman, GySgt Hank Head, Cpl Dave Hull, GySgt Mel Jones, Cpl Cece Malcomb, SSgt Bruce Martin, Sgt John Martin, Cpl Dan Moore, GySgt Ben Nereck, Sgt Cherilee Noyes, Sgt Jim Painter, Sgt Mike Ploog, GySgt Herb Richardson, LCpl John Ryan, Cpl Gary Scarborough, SSgt Steve Stibbens. Sgt Mike Sweeney, Sgt Paul Thompson, MSgt Wes Ward, Sgt Ray Wolf, SSgt

Rudy Woltner, and civilians Karl Schuon, Ronnie Lyons, Lou Lowery, Bob Davis, Bill Schneider, and Jim Hopewell.

Most newly arrived writers at *Leatherneck* Magazine were assigned as editor of the monthly "Sound Off" column. This was a feature column that answered questions sent in by our readers. My first column in April 1965 included the following under the heading, "TO THE POINT."

"I will get right to the point. Does the Marine Corps have Marines based in Israel? In what general capacity do these Marines serve? Could Marines volunteer for duty in Israel, and if so, what would be the length one would be there?"

My reply: "One 'get to the point' deserves another. Marines serve as security guards at the American Embassy in Tel Aviv. They may volunteer for a two-year tour of duty.-Ed"

I was also assigned the "Sports Shorts" column beginning in April 1965. My first column featured Staff Sergeant Les Ventura, an archer stationed at Camp Pendleton, California. SSgt Ventura had recently become the first man to record a perfect 400x400 score from the standing position at twenty-five yards.

My first *Leatherneck* Magazine feature article also appeared that month. It was titled "Dumpy Dan the Medal Man." It was about a hypothetical Marine who received the necessary assignments and had the good fortune over a two-year period to earn seven medals.

Gunny Mel Jones was the chief writer when I arrived. He had orders to 1st Marine Aircraft Wing in Iwakuni, Japan, and cleaned out his desk a short while later. SSgt Paul Berger, soon to be promoted to gunnery sergeant, was elevated to chief writer. Gunny Chris Evans, the man from whom I inherited the "Sound Off" column, received orders for the Marine Air Reserve Training Detachment in Norfolk. SSgt Bartlett, a Korean War veteran, arrived a couple of months earlier from the 1st Marine Corps District in Garden City, New York. We soon became the best of buddies.

Leatherneck Magazine was one of two magazines published by the Marine Corps Association, a private group outside the official Marine Corps structure. The Commandant of the Marine Corps was president of the association. *Leatherneck* Magazine was dedicated to the enlisted

Marine and his or her family. The *Marine Corps Gazette*, also published by the Association, was dedicated to the officer corps. The association and magazines exist today, but there are no active duty Marines assigned.

In addition to the monthly magazines, the Marine Corps Association publishes some military books and the *Guidebook for Marines*, a softback book containing military subjects every Marine is taught in boot camp. The *Guidebook* is often referred to as the Bible of basic Marine Corps subjects.

When I was with *Leatherneck* Magazine, stories were primarily self-generated by the writers. Occasionally, someone would call or write suggesting we write a story about this or that unit or Marine, but the writers did most of the brain storming. We would personally research a story idea and search back issues to see when or if a certain story had been done before. If five years had passed since a particular base or command had been featured, it was time to do it again. If a story idea was totally new, all the better.

At 8:15 a.m. on March 8, 1965, members of the 9th Marine Expeditionary Brigade landed on Red Beach in Da Nang, Vietnam. Unlike the opposed landings of World War II, when the Marines of Battalion Landing Team (BLT 3/9) hit the beach in Da Nang they were met by young Vietnamese girls bearing flowery leis, and four American soldiers with a large sign that read, "Welcome, Gallant Marines." Within two hours, BLT 1/3 began arriving at Da Nang Air Base. There were now thirty-five hundred U.S. Marines in Da Nang. Their mission—"Secure the Da Nang Air Base." This would free up some South Vietnamese soldiers for combat duty in the field.

SSgt Stibbens was the first *Pacific Stars & Stripes* correspondent to cover the war in Vietnam, beginning with the advisor phase in 1962. He was also *Stripes'* correspondent there in 1963. SSgt Stibbens was transferred to *Leatherneck* Magazine in 1964 and began another series of visits to Vietnam as a war correspondent.

Shortly after the Marines landed at Da Nang in March 1965,

SSgt Stibbens returned with his trusty Nikon F camera and 50mm lens. Photos he made in Vietnam in 1964 won him the title "Military Photographer of the Year." He won the competition again in 1965.

SSgt Bartlett relieved SSgt Stibbens as *Leatherneck* Magazine's combat correspondent in July 1965. Sgt Beardsley followed SSgt Bartlett in October and I followed Sgt Beardsley in January.

I had a footlocker full of story material by the end of March 1966, and SSgt Stibbens came back to relieve me—his fifth annual visit to cover the war in Vietnam; his last as a Marine—but he would be back. I'm getting ahead of myself.

My first brainstorming idea at the magazine sent me and photographer Cpl Scarbrough to Bermuda in April 1965 for a "Post of the Corps" feature about the Marine Barracks there. We took a "hop" to Bermuda from the Patuxent Naval Air Station in Patuxent, Maryland. The timing was perfect. It was Spring Break and the island was teaming with young college students. An annual festival was planned and it featured some Marines in their dress blue uniform and serving as escorts for the young ladies chosen as the pageant queen and princesses.

So much for good timing. While we were there, a civil war broke out in the Dominican Republic. U.S. Marines were dispatched to help evacuate Americans living in Santo Domingo the capital city. Gunny Berger was dispatched by *Leatherneck* Magazine to report on the situation. With all available American military passenger aircraft diverted to help with the evacuation effort, there were no planes for Cpl Scarbrough and me to catch a "hop" on to return home.

The per diem we had drawn for one week when we left the magazine was soon depleted. With no "free" government transportation available we were forced to contact the magazine and ask for money for a commercial flight home.

During the wait, there wasn't much we could do because we were almost broke. So, we got a couple of free passes from the Barracks to a local golf course. My only experience on a golf course came at the East

Potomac Golf Course at Haines Point, Washington, D.C., a few days before we left for Bermuda.

I purchased a box of twelve golf balls at the Henderson Hall PX for the trip. By the time we reached the ninth hole on Bermuda, I had only one ball left. All I could do was hook or slice the ball and I was constantly losing them. I sliced my drive off the tee at the ninth. When I reached the edge of the fence where I saw the ball go over, I saw it surrounded by several grazing cows. Then, as I watched, one of them wandered over, raised her tail and dropped a ten-inch patty on my ball. I didn't golf again until I was stationed at Misawa Air Base, Japan, ten years later. They had no cows there, only ravens.

The magazine wired us money for airfare and we caught a commercial flight home. The scheduled one-week trip to Bermuda ended two weeks after it began. *Leatherneck* Magazine coverage of Marines in Vietnam and the Dominican Republic began appearing in the August issue. Our story on Marine Barracks, Bermuda, was held until the September issue.

In June 1965, I was chosen to travel to Atlanta, Georgia, to retrieve a bottle of cognac placed in a bank vault there at the end of World War II. It belonged to the 1st Marine Division's "Last Man's Bottle Club." The object was that the last surviving Marine who served with the division during the Battle of Guadalcanal, August 1942–February 1943, would open the bottle and drink a toast to his departed comrades.

I made the trip in dress blues. Photos were made as I took possession of the bottle at the bank and when I arrived back in Washington, D.C. Before leaving Atlanta, I made an appearance on a local television news show. The young female moderator asked about the significance of the bottle and then asked me what my role was during the Battle of Guadalcanal. I was nineteen months old when the battle began. I looked at the announcer and in my sternest Marine Corps voice, replied "I was fighting diaper rash during that battle, ma'am." You could actually see the red creeping up her face—from neck to forehead.

I accepted the First Marine Division "Last Man's Bottle" from the president of Atlanta's First National Bank, Edward D. Smith.

William Kaduson, a public relations man for the Cognac Industries, accompanied me on the trip. He was full of praise when the mission was completed. Kaduson said in his letter to the 1st Marine Division Association,

> *Sergeant Bowen was absolutely tremendous in Atlanta and at the airport in Washington. He made an excellent impression on newspaper, radio and television people. Sergeant Bowen did his job well, and he couldn't have been more dedicated to the assignment. He's a good man.*

The last week of May and first week of June were devoted to marksmanship training at the Quantico rifle range. Every Marine was expected to maintain his proficiency as a shooter. When possible, we requalified with the rifle each year. This would be my second requalification since boot camp. My score of 221 with the M-14 permitted me to continue wearing my expert rifle badge.

I wrote a monthly series of one-page features in 1965 to let Marines know how they could earn a college degree by taking off-duty courses, and how to become an officer by taking advantage of special programs the Marine Corps offered. (Unfortunately, the uncertainty of my schedule from week to week prevented me from enrolling in any of the courses. So, my education continued to be of the "on the job" type.) At the same time, my "Sports Shorts" and "Sound Off" columns continued, along with features on such subjects as Marines assigned to the USS *America* (a new Navy aircraft carrier), the Marine Barracks in Philadelphia, and the Corps' birthplace at Tun Tavern near Philadelphia's New Hall complex.

Moose Hunt in Newfoundland, with men from Marine Barracks, Argentia and *Leatherneck* Magazine photographer LCpl John Ryan.

In November, LCpl Ryan, a photographer, and I went to Newfoundland, Canada, to do a story on the Marine Barracks at the U.S. Naval Base in Argentia. Part of our coverage included an overnight moose hunting trip to Terra Nova National Park near St. John's. It was my third "Post of the Corps" feature in 1965—all of them Marine Barracks.

CHAPTER 13

Baptism of Fire

*Some people live an entire lifetime wondering
if they've made a difference in the world,
Marines don't have that problem.*
~ Ronald Reagan, 40th President of the United States

As mentioned earlier, Sgt Beardsley's Vietnam assignment ended in January. I had been lobbying to be named his replacement. It was not a slam dunk. I had no combat experience as SSgt Stibbens, SSgt Bartlett, and Sgt Beardsley did when they were sent to Vietnam. My wife and I were expecting our second child in March, but the war could end at any time and no Marine writer worth his salt would pass up a chance to face the ultimate test—that of a combat correspondent.

Col Dickson understood. He approved my assignment, sat me down and gave me some advice from his days as a Marine combat correspondent on Guadalcanal. He was emphatic in that since I would be working side-by-side with a lot of civilian correspondents, I should help them when I could.

I wasted no time picking up my orders. On December 7, I had orders in hand authorizing transportation to Vietnam via government air, military air transport service, commercial air, or by rail. To get to Vietnam, I was authorized to visit Thailand, Taiwan, Wake Island, Japan, Guam, Hong Kong, Hawaii, the Philippines, and Okinawa.

The magazine sent two correspondents to Vietnam that month.

Sgt Burgoyne, an artist, had requested a brief assignment so he could capture some of the war on his sketch pad.

We flew commercially to Los Angeles and left the Marine Corps Air Station (MCAS) in El Toro, California, on January 2 and arrived at Futenma Air Facility, Okinawa, on January 4. The first available "hop" to Da Nang was scheduled for January 10, so we had six days to get reacquainted with "The Rock." At the top of my list was one of those two-hour treatments at the Paris barbershop on Gate Two Street outside Kadena Air Base. In the brief two years I had been away from Okinawa, prices had sky rocketed in the war climate. The haircut, shave, mudpack, and massage I had received for two dollars in 1962–1964, now cost five dollars. It was still worth the price so I coughed up a "fiver" and enjoyed the experience.

Sgt Burgoyne and I roamed the island while we were there—me making photographs and him sketching everything he saw. Water buffalo, children, old papasans and mamasans, and Okinawan shrines and buildings were the subject of his pen, ink, and charcoal sketches.

When the 10th rolled around we were at Futenma early. There were some delays and our C-130 flight did not leave until 2:30 p.m. We arrived at Da Nang at 7:15 p.m. and were assigned to Sub Unit #2, Headquarters Company, Headquarters Battalion, Third Marine Division for duty with the III Marine Amphibious Force. Sgt Beardsley met us at the passenger terminal and drove us to the Press Center in the AP jeep. That would be my home for the next three months while not in the field. Sgt Burgoyne was there for three weeks.

The following day, I checked in at III MAF and received orders authorizing unrestricted travel throughout Vietnam on *Leatherneck* Magazine matters. The travel orders noted that I had a secret clearance. III MAF supply was out of most of the clothing items and 7-82 gear (pack, cartridge belt, bayonet, poncho, a canteen) I needed. Supply did have a .45 caliber pistol, a small supply of ammunition, three clips, a clip holder, and a holster. Sgt Beardsley took me to the local black market on Da Nang's Doc Lap Street, not far from the Press Center, to get the rest of what I needed.

I was shocked to learn that the Marine Corps had a limited supply of clothing and equipment while they were readily available in town. I have since learned that this is often the case, no matter which war or which service. The "locals" always have what you need, be it clothing, military equipment, or a bottle of Jim Beam or Johnny Walker Black Label.

Sgt Beardsley left for home a few days after I arrived. He covered several major Marine operations while he was there including Harvest Moon and Black Ferret, both near Chu Lai south of Da Nang. Combat photographer Dickey Chapelle was killed during Operation Black Ferret. She was the first war correspondent killed in Vietnam. Sgt Beardsley was there and witnessed her death. Often described as having balls and wearing pearl earrings, Dickey loved her Marines and died as she would have wanted—wearing her combat boots . . . and her pearl earrings.

The Press Center was an old French villa, leased to the Marines. Colonel Tom Fields was the officer in charge when I arrived. The major news outlets had offices there and at least one correspondent. *Leatherneck* Magazine had a very close working relationship with the AP. When I arrived, George Esper was the AP man on the scene. We went on combat operations together, exchanged information on upcoming operations, and Esper never hesitated to loan me the AP jeep if it was sitting idle when I needed it.

Da Nang Press Center.

The Press Center was home for the Combat Information Bureau (CIB). There was an escort section with Marines standing by to accompany civilian correspondents on combat operations, a photo lab, and the staff of the III MAF weekly newspaper, the *Sea Tiger*. All Marine Corps press releases passed through the CIB for clearance and release. The Press Center also had a restaurant and a bar.

One day while visiting the 1st Marine Air Wing in search of story ideas I bumped into my old school buddy, Sonny Bice. He was assigned there as a military policeman. His primary duty was to guard the China Beach quarters of Lieutenant General Lewis Walt, Commanding General of the Third Marine Amphibious Force. A few days later I saw Bice at a Vietnamese USO show at Freedom Hill.

2nd Lieutenant Fred Tucker, a combat seasoned veteran of the Corps' involvement in the Dominican Republic in 1965, was a member of the CIB escort section. I was anxious to get into the field to cover my first combat action. 2ndLt Tucker, a newly promoted brown bar, was determined that my first trip to the field would not be my last. I told him I was planning to visit Captain R. J. Driver's Echo Company, 2nd Battalion, 9th Marine Regiment south of Da Nang. I had learned that one of his platoon leaders, Staff Sergeant Lester Evans, was going to conduct a routine patrol in the company's tactical area of responsibility (TAOR). I wanted to go on the patrol. 2ndLt Tucker said he would be by my side. I appreciated his concern.

Shortly after moving out in the vicinity of the small rural hamlet of Bich Nam (1), we came under fire. We were inside a hedgerow adjacent to a rice paddy when the first shot rang out and the leaves began fluttering to the ground. I hit the ground before any of the leaves. With camera in hand I began a low crawl to where the Marines had taken up positions to return the fire. 2ndLt Tucker saw my first reaction to combat. He approved and grabbed his M-1 carbine and joined the Marines on the defensive perimeter.

A short while later, a fireteam began moving out, through the rice paddy, toward a hedgerow on the other side where the first shots had come from. At one point, a Marine was hit while advancing across the field to our front. 2ndLt Tucker rushed out with the Corpsman to retrieve the wounded Marine.

I was busy making photos as 2ndLt Tucker worked with the Corpsman and helped bring the wounded Marine back to safety. I can recall 2ndLt Tucker asking the wounded Marine how he felt. "I'd feel a lot better if you'd remove your finger from the hole in my arm, Sir," the Marine replied.

It was my turn to wipe the egg off my face when I went to put a new roll of film in my camera. In a hurry to reload the camera earlier, I had failed to engage the sprockets in the film. There were no photos of 2ndLt Tucker's heroism. Lesson learned. It never happened again and I completed my coverage of the Vietnam War with more than ten thousand images.

Before leaving on my trip, the assistant editor-publisher of the magazine, Captain Jerry Kershner, called me aside and asked that I look up Captain Carl Reckewell, the commanding officer of Fox Company, 2nd Battalion, 9th Marine Regiment. They had served together at some point in their careers.

Capt Carl Reckewell (l) briefs LtGen Victor Krulak (c)
on the conduct of the war in his TAOR as
commanding officer of Fox 2/9, 1966.

Marines of Fox 2/9 were conducting Operation Big Lodge, a three-day search and clear operation in the company's TAOR south of Da

Nang when I paid a visit in mid-January. We made contact with the enemy that day and several Marines were wounded, giving me another opportunity to make photos of some "real" combat Marines in action.

Capt Reckewell was a Marine's Marine, the type of leader who got up close and personal with everything his Marines did. Whether engaging the enemy or taking care of his wounded Marines, Capt Reckewell was always on the scene.

One of the photos I made the day I accompanied Fox 2/9 was of First Lieutenant Franklin Cox, an artillery forward observer attached to the company. Sgt Burgoyne, the *Leatherneck* Magazine artist who accompanied me to Vietnam, later took that photograph, flipped it, and rendered it as a painting for the cover of the December 1966 issue of the magazine. In the painting, 1stLt Cox is holding a Christmas card. In 2010, McFarland & Company published *Lullabies for Lieutenants*, Cox's personal memoir of his time in Vietnam. The photo I made of him appears in his book.

1stLt Franklin Cox, Artillery Forward Observer with Fox 2/9.
Author of the award-winning *Lullabies for Lieutenants*,
a memoir about his time in Vietnam, 1965–1966.

My first combat story, featuring Echo 2/9, was titled "Fire and Maneuver." It was published in the June 1966 issue of *Leatherneck* Magazine, the same month Capt Reckewell of Fox 2/9 and his company walked into a minefield. Three Marines were killed and twenty-one, including Capt Reckewell, were wounded. Capt Reckewell lost a leg. His "up close and personal" approach to leadership ultimately ended his career.

Wounded Marine from Fox 2/9 gets speedy exit from the battlefield.

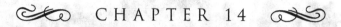

CHAPTER 14

Major Operations

It is easier to lead men to combat, stirring up
their passion than to restrain them and direct
them toward the patient labour of peace.
~ Andre Gide, French Writer and Humanist

My first two stories about major operations appeared in the June 1966 issue of *Leatherneck* Magazine.

Planning for Operation Double Eagle began in December 1966, after a large enemy force was detected along the I Corps and II Corps border in southern Quang Ngai Province. On January 27, correspondents at the Press Center were gathered together and asked if they'd like to go on an operation. The only stipulation was that they could not call their offices in Saigon and tell them where they were going. In fact, the correspondents were not even told where they were going.

I signed up along with Bob Ibrahim of UPI, Gus Jordan, a former Marine who was covering the war for the Navy *Times* newspaper, and several other correspondents. Jordan was wearing a multicolored tropical shirt—a strange way to dress for what we would later learn was to be the largest amphibious operation since Inchon during the Korean War. It would eventually be recorded as the largest amphibious landing of the Vietnam War. More than five thousand Marines were involved. Esper, AP correspondent, decided to sit this one out and pass along any news released at the Press Center after the operation got underway.

Operation Double Eagle—largest amphibious
operation of the Vietnam War.

We boarded choppers at the Da Nang Air Field and flew to the USS *Catamount*, (LSD-17), loaded with Marines and plying the South China Sea off the coast of Vietnam just south of Chu Lai. Marines from BLT 3/1 were lollygagging on the deck awaiting D-Day the following morning, The day was dreary when we awoke the following morning, January 28. Marines were scurrying about the deck cleaning their weapons and preparing for the amphibious landing scheduled to begin in an hour or two. The weather was not cooperating.

Mike boats were drilling holes in the sea near the *Catamount*, waiting for their call to come alongside and take on the Marines who would be climbing down the cargo nets hung over both sides of the LSD—port and starboard. It soon became apparent that both sides of the ship could not be used. The swells were just too high—the sea too rough.

When I climbed down the net, I noticed that the other correspondents were descending the same net. We were all going to wind up in the same Mike boat—everyone, including Jordan and his multicolored tropical shirt. As luck would have it, it was also the boat containing the commanding officer of Lima Company, 3rd Battalion, 1st Marine Regiment, Captain M. C. Pease. After all the training on

Okinawa and in the Philippines the company commander was leading a handful of Marines and a bunch of correspondents into combat. He glared at us as the Mike boat pulled away from the ship. If looks could have killed.

Other than the rain, huge seas, and dropping temperature, the landing was uneventful except that when we hit the beach we were met by AP photographer Eddie Adams. He had joined a Marine artillery unit placing a battery of guns on a hill overlooking the beach. He had been there for two days. So much for keeping the operation a secret.

Adams served in Korea as a Marine; a very talented photographer and a friend of many of the general officers in charge of the war. Adams met us on the beach with his customary grin spread from ear to ear and flipped us a one-finger salute. Two years later, Adams won a Pulitzer Prize for his photo of a South Vietnamese general executing a Vietcong prisoner on a Saigon street at the beginning of Tet, the Vietnamese New Year. Operation Double Eagle ended in mid-February. Three-hundred-twelve Vietcong and soldiers of the North Vietnam Army were killed. The operation also claimed the lives of one hundred twenty Allied soldiers. Two days later, the Marines launched Double Eagle II, about seventeen miles north of Chu Lai near the city of Tam Ky.

Operation Double Eagle II.

Warrant Officer Jim Smith of the CIB briefed the correspondents on Double Eagle II. He said the operation would involve four battalions. Marines from the Da Nang area arrived by truck convoy. I was on one of the trucks. The roads were so rough that screws in my Mamiya C-3 camera jarred loose and jammed the camera's focusing track. Luckily, I had my Nikon F camera with me so all was not lost. Operation Double Eagle II ended on February 28. No Marines were killed. The enemy lost one hundred twenty combatants.

Operation New York was a five-day sweep east of Phu Bai, a village just north of Da Nang. It began February 27 and ended March 3. It was conducted by the 2nd Battalion, 1st Marine Regiment and a South Vietnamese Army unit, supported by Marine helicopters from HMM-163. Fifteen Marines and ARVN were killed. The enemy lost one hundred twenty-two dead. Photos I made on the day I covered the operation were used to illustrate several "theme" pieces I later wrote for *Leatherneck* Magazine.

Marines of 2nd Battalion, 9th Marines board chopper at Tam Key for a short hop to the battle during Operation Eagle II.

Operation Utah was next up, about halfway between Da Nang and Chu Lai. In fact, it involved the same field commander that led Marines in battle during Operation Harvest Moon in November and December 1965, and Double Eagle II in February 1966. Brigadier General Jonas M. Platt, CG of Task Force Delta. Lieutenant Colonel Leon Utter, commanding officer of 2/7, played a principle role and earned his second Silver Star Medal within five months.

AP Correspondent George Esper (second from right) interviews
BGen Jonas Platt who has arrived on scene to evaluate
the conduct of Operation Utah, 1966.

The target was the 21st Regiment of the North Vietnamese Army. They were dug in on Hill 50. When the four-day battle ended on March 7, ninety-eight Marines and thirty South Vietnamese soldiers had been killed. The enemy lost six hundred men, many of whom were killed in the underground tunnel complex deep inside Hill 50.

A few days later, I flew to Saigon to make photos and gather information on Marines assigned to guard the U.S. Embassy. While there, I accompanied Eddie Adams on an assignment to make photos of the execution of a war profiteer of Chinese descent. The firing squad execution was scheduled for public viewing at Saigon's Central Market. It was timed for around midnight on March 13 when most of the city was sleeping. Adams and I had decided that when the time came he would focus his attention on the actual execution. I would make photos of the spectators.

AP photographer Eddie Adams gets cameras
ready for an execution in Saigon, 1966.

The Saigon police, known as White Mice because of their white uniforms, arrived at Central Square with the handcuffed prisoner, Ta Vinh. They escorted him quickly to a wall where several poles were poking out of the ground in front of a stack of sandbags. He was tied to one of the poles. The police vehicles pivoted to face the onlookers and turned their bright lights on. It was difficult to see anything, much less get a good photograph of the execution. That was Adam's problem.

When the police arrived with Ta Vinh, his wife and several children began struggling to reach him from their position about three hundred yards away. The only possible way for them to get to their doomed husband and father was by crawling down the center of a roll of concertina wire, stretched out to prevent anyone from entering the Square. Their hands, arms, and faces were bloodied from making contact with the razor-sharp wire. They were halfway through the barrier when shots rang out and they slumped to the ground just as their husband and father did. Only he was dead. I am sure they have never forgotten that incident. I still remember it vividly, but the photos I made were misplaced and I have no visual documentation.

One of the daily rituals of the correspondents in Saigon was to attend the "Five O'Clock Follies," the daily news briefings given by the Military Assistance Command, Vietnam (MACV). I wasn't at the briefing, but a few days before the war profiteer's execution, one of the AP correspondents told me my name had come up during the briefing that day. At some point between the daily report of casualties and number of bombs dropped, the briefer said, "We received a Red Cross message from the Da Nang Press Center. Sergeant Bowen of *Leatherneck* Magazine is down here working on some stories. If anyone sees him, let him know he has a daughter, born March 10. Mother and daughter, are doing fine."

I was staying at the Continental Palace Hotel. When I returned to my room the evening of March 12, the following message was waiting: "Please call Major Reilly at 25565." Major Reilly repeated the message announced during the daily briefing, but added that my daughter was 7 pounds and 10 ounces, and was born at the Portsmouth Naval Hospital in Portsmouth, Virginia. I wrapped up my business in Saigon as quickly as I could and rushed back to Da Nang.

My three-month tour was rapidly coming to an end. My replacement, SSgt Stibbens already had his bags packed and was making final plans for his sixth trip to Vietnam to cover the war. I had made some lifelong friends and acquaintances: Joe Galloway of UPI would later write *We Were Soldiers Once . . . and Young.* Lieutenant Frank Cox would write *Lullabies for Lieutenants.*

AP's Esper stayed in Vietnam ten years and ended his time there as the Saigon Bureau Chief before retiring and returning to his alma mater, West Virginia University, Morgantown, to teach journalism. He died in 2012. Then, there was Pulitzer Prize-winning AP photographer Adams.

Adams once told me he was afraid every time he went on an operation. But, that it was that fear that kept him alert and alive. Adams survived thirteen wars. He died of Lou Gehrig's disease in 2004.

CHAPTER 15

Back to the World

War! that mad game the world so loves to play.
~ Jonathan Swift, Irish Satirist

My introduction to combat had been an exciting adventure. My instructors at boot camp and at Camp Geiger's advanced infantry training had taught me well. I had survived the ultimate test. My editors were pleased with my reporting. The photo director at the magazine complimented my photographs. I had a new daughter, Donna. I was ready to go home—back to the world, as we said in Vietnam.

I left Da Nang on March 21 on a flight to Okinawa. From there, I flew to MCAS in El Toro, arriving there on the 24th. A commercial flight to Washington, D.C., a few days to get reacquainted with my family—especially my new daughter, Donna—and I reported back to the magazine on March 25. I had been away from home for eighty-nine days, eighty of them in Vietnam, mostly covering combat operations.

Before leaving for Vietnam, I had asked a Navy doctor about a festering spot beneath my left eye. He diagnosed the sore as a cyst that would go away in time. "Nothing to be overly concerned about," he said.

By the time I returned home from Vietnam, the top of the sore had come off and it looked like an erupting volcano. I went back to the same doctor, who now said it looked like a basal cell and should be removed. Surgery at Bethesda Naval Medical center in Maryland was prescribed. The cancer was removed, a piece of skin snipped from behind my left ear was grafted beneath my eye. There has been no recurrence.

Sgt Beardsley and I spent a lot of our spare time fishing. Blueback herring migrated up the Potomac each April to spawn and Sgt Beardsley and I frequently fished the Potomac River near McLean, Virginia. We used treble hooks to snag the herring. Then we would remove their guts and gills and use them to catch huge channel catfish. One day I snagged a ground hog trying to swim across the swirling Potomac. I took it home in my burlap bag full of fish and gave him to a neighbor who said he liked ground hog stew. I've always suspected he released him in the woods near our home.

One morning on the Potomac, a man fishing from a rock about fifty yards down river, asked if we had the time. Sgt Beardsley responded. A few minutes later we heard a big splash. We looked back to where the man had been fishing. He was not there. His body floated to the surface near Fletcher's Boat House a few days later. The Potomac was narrow and especially rough where we fished, with fast moving eddies swirling around huge boulders that stuck out of the water. We seldom went there after the drowning incident. We discovered Goose Creek and bass fishing near Leesburg, Virginia.

I was back on the road in June for a story on a Marine reserve refueling unit in Little Creek, Virginia. Later that month, LCpl Ryan and I traveled to Marine Corps Air Station, Cherry Point, North Carolina, to report on a reconnaissance squadron based there. Our story, "Eye in the Sky," was published in the October issue of the magazine.

While there, I took a brief course on how to eject from a jet while in flight. I was scheduled to return to Vietnam in 1967 and I wanted to do a story on close air support. To make it more realistic, I hoped to fly in every combat plane in the Marine Corps inventory except those that had only a pilot. To fly in a jet, I would need to be certified as having undergone ejection seat training. You received a card after this training that Marines called an "oh my ass" card.

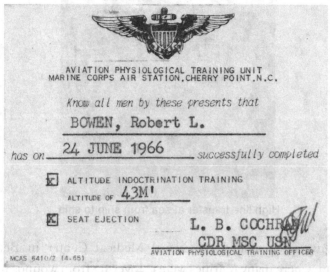

"Oh My Ass" Flight Card.

In August, I accompanied the National Security Commission of the American Legion on a trip to Little Creek, Virginia, where we boarded a Navy ship and sailed to a position off the coast of Camp Lejeune and Jacksonville, North Carolina. While at sea, we witnessed drills to avoid torpedoes, and saw how men and equipment transfer from ship to ship by way of a high line transfer. From there we flew by helicopters to Camp Lejeune to observe Marines in mock combat.

High line transfer at sea from ship to ship.

In August, I visited the Naval Medical Center in Bethesda, Maryland, where many Marines were recovering from wounds received in Vietnam. Private First Class Jim Patridge was one of the wounded. He had lost both legs when a "bouncing betty" exploded while on patrol with H 2/9. Even at that, he was lucky. One Marine was killed.

The Commandant of the Marine Corps, General Wallace M. Greene, Jr., was there that day. Dubbed "Operation Appreciation," the day of recognition was organized by the General Douglas MacArthur Post 1853 of the Catholic War Veterans, and included a trip to a Washington Senators ball game for those able to make the trip.

Maryland Congressman Hervey G. Machen saw the article I wrote about Operation Appreciation in the August issue of *Leatherneck* Magazine and had it inserted in the August 10, 1966 Congressional Record.

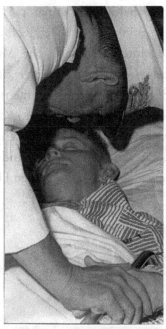

Gen Wallace M. Greene, Jr., CMC, whispers a word of encouragement to wounded Marine PFC Jim Patridge at Bethesda Naval Hospital, 1966.

In November, my article on Marine Barracks 8th & I, "The Home of the Corps," received favorable reviews as did my whimsical historical piece on Lucy Brewer, rumored to have served in the Marine Corps during the War of 1812—disguised as a male Marine. My story was titled "Musket for My Lady."

Marine Barracks, 8th & I Evening Parade.

Leatherneck Magazine held a Christmas party each year and the commandant was always invited. Gen Greene, the 23rd Commandant, attended in 1966. He chitchatted with the Marines assigned and complimented the writers for their coverage of the war. When he learned that I was scheduled to return in January, he pulled me aside and said there was one group of Marines that had not yet received any coverage in the magazine. I asked him which group. "The dogs—scout dogs and sentry dogs. They're doing an outstanding job in Vietnam," Gen Greene said. I knew an implied order when I heard one. "Consider it done, Sir," I said.

CHAPTER 16

On the Road Again

For a war correspondent to miss an invasion
is like refusing a date with Lana Turner.
~ Robert Capa, Hungarian Combat Correspondent

I picked up my orders to return to Vietnam on December 28, flew to the West Coast and on to Okinawa and Vietnam, arriving in Da Nang on January 7, 1967. On the flight from El Toro to Okinawa, I was seated across from a scout dog making his first trip to the battlefield. It was as if the Commandant was providing a constant reminder of my promise to write a story about the dogs. The German shepherd snarled, growled, and barked at me the entire flight.

My story list for 1967 contained only three ideas. The Commandant's dog story, a story on close air support (I had my "oh my ass" card safely tucked away in my wallet), and one about LtGen Walt, Commanding General of III MAF and I Corps. I was hoping to complete the Walt piece in time to make the April issue. Managing Editor Schuon had agreed to that scheduling—if I was quick. That would be my first story.

I made arrangements to meet with LtGen Walt shortly after arriving, getting settled in at the Press Center, scrounging up the equipment I would need, and introducing myself to an entirely new group of correspondents who occupied the old villa.

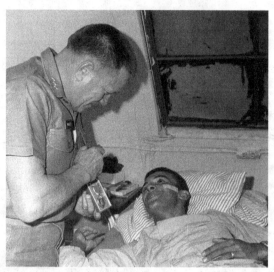

LtGen Lewis W. Walt presented a Purple Heart medal to a Marine recovering from his wounds in the Da Nang hospital, 1967.

Bob Gassaway was the new AP man. Gassaway was my age, but he was huge! He stood six feet, four inches tall and weighed more than three hundred pounds. When he ventured to take a hop on a helicopter he was asked to move to the center of the chopper, especially the small Hueys. Gassaway became my best friend on this trip.

LtGen Lewis W. Walt always had time to answer a few questions from Bob Gassaway, AP, February 1967.

The actor, Glenn Ford, arrived in Vietnam in January. He was there to gather footage for a training film titled "Global Marine." Ford had served as a Marine sergeant during World War II. In 1967, he held the commission of a Naval Reserve commander.

Ford spent a week with LtGen Walt in Northern Vietnam. I was with them for most of their visits to Marines in the field: Phu Bai, Camp Carroll, the Rockpile, Dong Ha, Cam Lo, Khe Sahn, Con Thien, and smaller camps occupied by Marines, Army Special Forces, Australian soldiers, and the South Vietnamese Army. We flew everywhere we went in the general's Huey helicopter.

LtGen Lewis W. Walt talking to the pilot of his helicopter.

LtGen Lewis W. Walt briefs his commanders
in an underground bunker at Camp Carroll.

LtGen. Lewis W. Walt had a conversation with a Marine
at the Rockpile. "What are you digging," the general
asked the Marine. "A crapper," the Marine replied.
"That's a mighty fine crapper," LtGen Walt said.

Later I learned that LtGen Walt had been wounded riding in his chopper the previous October. According to UPI, a Vietcong bullet pierced his helicopter while flying over Marines engaged in combat in Quang Tri Province. The bullet broke through the Plexiglas windshield and a piece of metal cut the general's face. At the time, it was said LtGen Walt was the highest ranking officer wounded in Vietnam.

I spent a week writing the story. When I reached a point where I needed a piece of information I did not have, I would call the general's aide and arrange to pay a quick visit with another question. On one occasion, I asked LtGen Walt if he had any regrets about the war in Vietnam or his conduct of the war. "I can only say," he said "that if I didn't believe in what we're doing here, with all my heart, I wouldn't be able to live with the lives that have been taken and the effort that has been expended."

LtGen. Lewis W. Walt said, "If I didn't believe in what we're doing here, with all my heart, I wouldn't be able to live with the lives that have been taken and the effort that has been expended."

I finished the story, wrote captions for the photos I wanted to illustrate the piece, then crafted a three-word title for the story. Everyone I had spoken to while gathering information for the story had commented on how much the lowest ranking "grunt" in Vietnam respected LtGen Walt. Grunt was a well-respected term to apply to a combat Marine enlisted man. So, the title I put on the article was "Three-Star Grunt."

My editors hit the ceiling. "You can't call a three-star general a grunt," they said in a tersely worded message. "Give us another title." I took the ferry to III MAF headquarters on the other side of the Han River. I walked into the general's office and sat down outside his door where he could see me when the door opened. I told the aide I needed to see LtGen Walt one last time.

A short while later, the door opened, the general saw me sitting there and asked the aide what I needed. I had not told the aide, so he told LtGen Walt I needed to ask him another question. LtGen Walt beckoned me in, asked what I needed, and when he learned of the brouhaha my title had caused at the magazine, he chuckled and said not to worry, he would take care of it.

On my previous "last" visit to see the general, we had flown in his helicopter to Hill 55 where I made a series of color photos for consideration as the cover for the magazine in which my story would appear. While on that trip, I had told LtGen Walt that I planned to title the story "Three-Star Grunt." He was pleased.

The story appeared as I had titled it in the April issue. The following month, *Life* Magazine published a cover story about LtGen Walt titled, "Big Lew Walt."

CHAPTER 17

The Air Was Ours

When a Marine is wounded, surrounded,
hungry or low on ammo, he looks to the sky.
He knows the choppers are coming.

~ Anonymous

I had been taking flights in combat aircraft every chance I had since arriving in Vietnam—Huey helicopters, UH-34Ds, CH-46s, CH-53s, C-130s, and the O-1E "Bird Dog." The flights were primarily to make photos for the "close air support" feature I had planned.

CH-46 helicopter disgourges its load of fighting Marines
during Operation Meade River, 1968.

115

I arrived at the Marine Corps airbase at Chu Lai on January 25. The *MAG-13* weekly announced that "Bob Bowen, a staff writer/photographer for the 'Leatherneck,' arrived 25 January to commence gathering material for an article 'Marine Close Air Support.' Bob will be in the Group area for about six days and visiting each squadron. Maximum Command assistance is desired." So, with that introduction, I began to work on my goal of flying in a jet on a combat mission to complete my research for the close air support story.

Marines of Fox 2/9 await their turn to board helicopters that will take them to the battlefield during Operation Double Eagle II, February 1966.

I explained my mission to the group commander and showed him my "oh my ass" card. Before he would okay a backseat ride in a Phantom he wanted me to experience the "thrill" of flying backseat in the smaller TF-9J Cougar. Several of the two-seater Korean War-era Grumman jets were maintained by Headquarters and Maintenance Squadron-23. The plan was for us to "drill holes in the sky" over Chu Lai for an hour or so and then I would be given the opportunity to take the "stick" and actually fly the jet for a few minutes.

Author preparing to fly in the backseat of a TF-9J Cougar.

We had no sooner cleared the airstrip on January 27, when we were assigned a mission to fly cover for three helicopters carrying three 105mm artillery pieces to a location south of Chu Lai. "You watch the port side," the pilot said. "I'll watch the starboard side."

This arrangement worked fine for the first three or four checks. If I had one chopper on the left, the pilot saw two choppers on the right, or vice versa. The time came when the numbers we called out did not equal three. When that happened the pilot flipped the Cougar over and went searching for the missing chopper.

Oops! There went my breakfast. It filled up the breathing regulator I was wearing. I sucked it back in, rechewed and swallowed as fast as I could. I had borrowed the regulator from the squadron commander. He would be incensed. No Phantom flight for me, I decided. I later learned that I had lasted longer than the commander had anticipated and that he had given me an old, but serviceable, regulator for my virgin flight.

117

The next morning, I again climbed into a flight suit, flight harness, helmet, and all other necessary flight gear, only this time I was going up in an F-4. My gaff with the TF-9J had been expected and was forgiven.

Selfie of the author on bombing run in backseat of an F-4.

We streaked down the airstrip at Chu Lai, lifted off, circled the field once or twice to gain altitude, then headed to the northern-most reaches of South Vietnam. For this flight, I was assigned as copilot for Lieutenant Colonel Avery Talbert. Our Phantom, and the one flying alongside, were both fully loaded with rockets and bombs. Our mission was to fly around and be ready to zoom in and drop our ordinance if and when called on.

About thirty minutes of flying circles in the sky and we were assigned a mission. Some Marines on the ground had made contact with a large enemy force in northern I-Corps near the DMZ and needed our help. There was no O-1E Bird Dog to guide us to our target. The Marines had smoke grenades and they were used to show us where to drop our bombs. My pilot swooped down, dropped his bombs on target, pulled smoothly out of his dive and we flew back to Chu Lai. Our bird had no more eggs.

Phantom F-4 on bombing run over northern I-Corps.

On February 1, I was flying with the O-1E Bird Dogs from their home at the Marble Mountain Airfield near Da Nang. Lieutenant Colonel Jack Evans was commander of the detachment. A call came in to support an operation south of Da Nang. "You come with me," LtCol Evans said, pointing in my direction. So, I donned a flight suit, grabbed my camera, and followed him to his military Cessna. I would be his designated copilot on this flight.

An O-1E Cessna Bird Dog approaches the future landing zone for a company of combat Marines.

LtCol Evans explained the mission to me. We would be guiding three flights of jets—each flight stacked on top of another—to their target that morning. The mission was to clear a landing zone for helicopters carrying Marines into combat—close air support at its finest. Operation Independence was kicking off. I would join the Marines on the ground for that operation five days later.

An F-4 Phantom gains altitude after dropping its payload
of Napalm on the hamlet of Minh Tan (2) during
Operation Independence, February 1967.

LtCol Evans was in constant radio contact with the first F-4 flight leader. He gave his position, went into a nose dive, and fired his two 2.75mm white phosphorous rockets to mark the target. The first flight of jets followed quickly and dropped their load of bombs on the chosen chopper landing zone.

We had already used our rockets, so when the second flight dropped out of the clouds to be guided to the target, LtCol Evans directed my attention to several colored smoke grenades attached to the inside of my door. "Pick one," he said. "What color did you choose?" he asked. "Yellow," I said.

"Okay," here's what we're going to do," he said. "On my command, you will reach your arm out the window as far as you can and throw the smoke grenade straight down."

Sounded easy enough.

LtCol Evans made contact with the flight leader. He told him he was out of WP rockets but that he would mark the target with a yellow smoke grenade. The Phantom pilot said he understood. We flew to our drop point, LtCol Evans commanded "Watch my wings" at which point he jostled the wings rapidly up and down, first left then right, three or four times. The Phantom pilot saw us. He was then told to "Watch my smoke"—my command to throw the smoke grenade. I did, and immediately followed the smoke with my breakfast. The rapid movement of the wings when my stomach was programmed to go forward had been too much for this Marine.

I used a purple smoke grenade for the third and final bomb run to clear the landing zone. I knew what to expect that time and what was left of my breakfast remained in my stomach.

CHAPTER 18

Operation Independence

For over 221 years our Corps has done
two things for this great Nation.
We make Marines, and we win battles.

~ General Charles C. Krulak,
31st Commandant of the Marine Corps

Operation Independence kicked off shortly after I completed the piece on Gen Walt. This search and destroy operation was conducted in Quang Nam Province, west of An Hoa. It lasted only nine days, February 1–9. It involved Marines from the 1st, 4th, 5th, and 26th Regiments along with a platoon of Reconnaissance Marines, some South Vietnamese Army units, an Army Special Forces unit, and a Marine Combined Action Company. Colonel Robert "Bob" M. Richards, commander of the 9th Marine Regiment, was in charge of the operation.

The focus of Operation Independence was a portion of the North Vietnamese R-20 Main Force Battalion and the Q-16 local Vietcong Force Company.

Gunnery Sergeant Lee Witconis, editor of the Marine's *Sea Tiger* newspaper, and I were relaxing at the Da Nang Press Center on Sunday morning, February 5. We learned of some heavy fighting and enemy being captured on Operation Independence some twenty miles southwest of Da Nang, so we arranged to accompany a resupply helicopter to where the action was. Shortly after arriving half a dozen

Vietcong and North Vietnamese Army detainees were brought to the top of a ridge where they were interrogated and processed before being flown by a UH-34D helicopter to Da Nang for further questioning.

Col Bob Richards had operational
control of Operation Independence.

Marines of Fox 2/26 held the ridgeline and we soon began walking down, across a valley towards a hedgerow that bordered a wide rice paddy. On the other side of the paddy, the hamlet of Minh Tan (2)—the target of our attack—could be seen being softened up by an assortment of jets from the 1st Marine Air Wing.

As Gunny Witconis and I approached the edge of the rice paddy, we saw a group of Marines clustered at the base of a small pagoda nestled adjacent to the hedgerow that defined the edge of the paddy. I began walking towards where a Marine sat smoking a cigarette, waiting for the jets to finish their job so the assault across the rice paddy could begin.

"Hold it," he said as I began approaching him. "We've found a couple booby traps in the area. If you walk straight to me, you'll be okay. Don't deviate. Walk straight and you'll be okay."

I had taken three steps when my right foot sank four inches beneath the surface of the ground. I stood there, balancing precipitously on one foot, while the Marine who had been guiding me, walked slowly forward, knelt down and began cautiously probing around my right foot with his bayonet.

"There's a wire under your foot," he said, "but fortunately your foot has not pushed down on it. Very slowly, I want you to raise your foot and step backwards."

I followed his advice, struggling to maintain my balance. Two more backward steps and I was clear of the danger zone. But, despite having two cameras hanging around my neck, I was too keyed up to memorialize the event in photos.

The Marine then slowly returned to where he had been sitting at the edge of the pagoda and began carefully probing the ground. It wasn't long before he found a 105mm artillery round, no doubt a dud when it was first fired by cannon cockers of an 11th or 12th Marine Artillery Battery, but still chock full of dangerous explosives. It was fused and connected to the wire that had been beneath my right foot.

After the jets had finished their job of softening up Minh Tan (2), and the men of Fox 2/26 were halfway across the rice paddy, engineers detonated the artillery round that had my name on it. The pagoda and the knoll it sat on, belched skyward with a roar. My knees trembled and I slowly knelt in the paddy and uttered a prayer of thanks.

Ambush!

125

All was quiet as we stepped out of the rice paddy and into the hamlet of Minh Tan (2). I had just taken a few photos of two water buffalo, a female and her calf, when all hell broke loose. To quote my story that appeared in *Leatherneck* Magazine.

Foxtrot was about midway through the hamlet now. If Charlie Cong was still in the area, he would have to show his hand soon; Foxtrot was getting too close to his lair.

Too close.

Bang!

The shot broke through the air with a sickening sound.

More shots followed in rapid succession. Charlie Cong had been pushed as far as he was going to be pushed. His back was to the river and he was fighting like a caged rat.

"Corpsman!"

A Marine had been hit. Then another. Charlie Cong couldn't be seen, but the bullets he was throwing were finding their marks.

Foxtrot answered the fire.

"Over there! They're in that treeline!"

The air was ablaze with hot lead. Leaves dropped from trees; bamboo toppled over as if felled by an ax; dust filled the air as the bullets danced across the ground, searching, searching. And, Marines fell.

We need a med evac! Somebody get a med evac!

Where's that radio man?"

Suddenly, what had been feared most, happened. Fire from the rear. Charlie Cong was firing from the rear! He had been in those bomb shelters when the Marines came through, only too deep for the sensitive nose of a scout dog to detect.

Pray, baby, pray!

"They've got us surrounded!"

Pray, baby, pray.

Thud!

"Corpsman!"

Foxtrot was in up to their butts. Sweat fell in torrents. Rifle barrels became hot from continuous firing.

"Who's got some ammo?"

"Here! Here comes a magazine!"

"Where'd it go? I can't see it!"

"It fell on the path! Can you edge your arm out and get it?"

Zing!

"Man, I can't reach it!"

"I'm sorry. Damn, I'm sorry!"

The firing slackened. A hand crept out of the hedgerow, reaching for the magazine.

"I got it!"

"Give 'em hell!"

Fox 2/26 Marine running to the action
when the ambush is launched.

Running to the action.

Gunny Witconis rushed to the side of the nearest wounded Marine,

Corporal Melvin G. Moffett, and began helping the Corpsman who appeared out of nowhere. Cpl Moffett had just been appointed a squad leader that morning. The Corpsman was treating his first combat casualty.

My first instinct was to reach for my weapon, but my .45 caliber pistol would be of little use in an ambush where you could not see your attackers. So, I holstered the pistol and began making photos.

Several more Marines were hit before we could organize and call for a medevac chopper. Gunny Witconis and I accompanied the wounded Marines to the medical facility at An Hoa. Several captured North Vietnamese soldiers and Vietcong guerrillas were there being treated for their wounds.

Marine is hit. Corpsman and combat correspondent
Gunny Lee Witconis to his aid.

Walking wounded.

Walking and carried wounded.

Marine hits the deck searching for a target after
VC ambush Fox 2/26 in Minh Tan (2).

A gathering place for the wounded
of Fox 2/26 on Operation Independence.

Cpl Moffett had died during his flight to An Hoa. All of the bleeding was from the inside of his thigh, and that was believed to be the point of entry for the bullet that hit him. Wrong. He had been hit in his stomach, on the clasp of his cartridge belt. The bullet had ricocheted through his spleen, carrying pieces of the belt's brass hook with it, and on down his leg where it exited his inner thigh. The Navy doctor on duty at An Hoa said there was so much internal damage Cpl Moffett would have died even if he had been shot while on the operating table. The doctors and Corpsmen had no sooner completed working on

Cpl Moffett than a chopper arrived carrying several more wounded Vietcong and North Vietnamese Army soldiers. It reminded me of stories I had heard about the medical profession in every war America has ever fought, from the Revolutionary War to the present. Something called the Hippocratic Oath kicks in.

When the operation ended, one hundred fifty-three enemy were dead—another one hundred ninety were believed to have been killed. We had captured one hundred ninety-three, both North Vietnamese Army and Vietcong. Thirty-nine NVA had rallied to the South Vietnam side. Nine Marines were killed during Operation Independence. Forty-two were wounded.

After the battle, I wrote a brief news item at Gunny Witconis' request for the February 15 issue of the *Sea Tiger.* It was headlined, "Foxtrot won't soon forget Minh Tan (2), By: Sgt. Bob Bowen, Leatherneck Magazine."

Author's lofty interview of Marine high above rice paddies
surrounding the Marble Mountain complex.

After writing a much lengthier piece for the magazine, I retreated to the mountaintop lair where three artillery forward observers from the 1st Battalion, 11th Artillery Regiment, and two radar beacon operators made their home. It was the tallest (118.4 meters) of a cluster of five marble and limestone hills that make up the Marble Mountain complex, not far from Da Nang. The Marines' job was to keep a constant watch on the area beneath their "eagle's nest." The Marine's Marble Mountain Airfield was nearby. So was the Force Logistics Command (FLC) and III MAF Headquarters.

Marble Mountain Outpost near Da Nang.

Claymore mines were strategically placed at all avenues of approach, and I'm not aware of any enemy ever reaching the lofty position. The Vietcong were rumored to maintain a hospital in one of the many caves in the complex, and if that's true the Marines and Vietcong had learned to practice peaceful coexistence, at least on this piece of terrain.

I spent two days on Marble Mountain. The position was established shortly after the Marines arrived in Vietnam in 1965. Observers there in September of that year had witnessed the firefight and capture of Marine PFC Bobby Garwood, a 3rd Marine Division driver, who became lost while going to pick up an officer. PFC Garwood learned of the operation after he returned home from Vietnam in 1979. My story on the Marble Mountain Men was published in May. The article on Operation Independence appeared in June.

Maple Mountain Outpost near De Vent

CHAPTER 19

The Commandant's Request

Let slip the dogs of war.
~ Shakespeare in *Julius Caesar*

Now, to focus on the Commandant's canines.

In February 1967, the Marine Corps had fifty-six dogs in Vietnam. They included both scout dogs and sentry dogs. Each variety was trained for a specific mission. They were kept at Camp Kaiser near Da Nang. The camp was named for the first scout dog killed in Vietnam.

All war dogs received three months of intensive training at Fort Benning, Georgia. The first Marine scout dog arrived in Vietnam in March 1966. They were assigned to the 1st Military Police Battalion, 1st Marine Division.

The dogs were "on call" weapons of war. First Lieutenant Ron Neubauer was the commander of both scout and sentry dog platoons. He explained that requests to use the dogs could be for as little as two hours or as long as five days. "Once a unit uses a dog, they'll come back again," 1stLt Neubauer said.

One Marine, the "point," normally leads the way for a platoon on patrol. When a dog is assigned to a platoon, the point, is made up of a scout dog and his handler. Their job is to flush out any danger that might lurk ahead. The tools they employ consist of a nose that can smell sixty times better than the average Marine, two eyes that can see twenty times better, and two ears that can hear forty times better. The handler is armed with a .45 pistol. The dog has sharp teeth.

Marine handler directs his scout dog to check out a bunker.

The dogs seldom use their teeth in their work, except to show them. "We don't want our dogs to be vicious," 1stLt Neubauer said. "They need to be aggressive—a controlled aggressiveness."

Each dog had its' own handler. On February 3, I accompanied Lance Corporal Steve Beezy and his scout dog, "Gary," on Operation Independence. (It was the second time I had gathered material for a magazine piece associated with that nine-day major combat operation. The first time was two days earlier in an O-1E "Bird Dog" Cessna.) Before leaving Camp Kaiser, I decided to test the dog—or at least get an idea what a Vietcong hiding in a hole might experience if a scout dog found him while on patrol.

Cpl Steve Beezy and his scout dog, Gary, on the prowl.

The dog training area at Camp Kaiser included several "spider" holes and tunnels, similar to those used by the Vietcong. I tested the strength of a dog's leash, measured it, then crawled backwards into one of the tunnels with my camera. Cpl Beezy commanded "sic 'em" and his German shepherd attacked. Having previously checked the depth of the tunnel and the length of Gary's leash, I knew just how far I had to retreat. Cpl Beezy knew just when to halt Gary's advance. The Vietcong did not have the advantage of that kind of preplanning.

The military used only German shepherds in Vietnam. They are intelligent, fairly easy to train, and they adapt to changing surroundings and climates. Most important, the German shepherd is devoted to its handler.

What the enemy saw when the scout dog found him.

Cpl Steve Beezy and Gary cross a stream
during Operation Independence, February 1967.

Sergeant Marvin Wiley and his dog Kelley were on Operation Dover near Chu Lai in October 1966. Sgt Wiley and Kelley were on point with a patrol from A Company, 1/5. Suddenly Kelley veered to the right. "I kept walking straight," Sgt Wiley recalled, "because Kelley had not alerted on anything. I hit the edge of a punji pit and it gave 'way. I pulled all my weight over to my right leg, stopped, and called for the engineers."

The engineers found an ingeniously designed death trap consisting of four grenades, one in each corner of the punji pit, and a 105mm round in the bottom of the pit. The pins of the grenades were connected to wires crossing the pit. Pressure on the wire would have pulled the pins, setting off the grenades. The concussion would have set off the artillery round. Kelley got a "good doggie" treat that night.

The Marine's weekly newspaper in Vietnam, the *Sea Tiger*, frequently carried stories about the exploits of the scout and sentry dogs. The January 15, 1967 issue reported that "Woton, a German police scout dog, 1st MP Bn., 1st MarDiv, is a hero in the eyes of 1st Recon Bn. Marines. They credit the dog with saving them from ambushes six times during patrol deep in VC territory." Woton's handler, PFC Nick Wills, said that on December 30, 1966, Woton was wounded after warning the Marines of one ambush.

The following year, the *Sea Tiger* reported on a scout dog and his handler assigned to the 3rd Military Police Battalion, a unit of the FLC. Sergeant Frank Spano, and his dog, Lobo, successfully jumped from a C-130 transport plane while undergoing parachute training on Okinawa.

Sgt Spano and Lobo regularly accompanied Marines of the 3rd Force Reconnaissance Battalion., in Vietnam. The Reconnaissance Marines frequently jumped into their operations and by becoming parachute qualified, the scout dog team would be able to accompany them on the parachute insertions as well.

The Army announced in early 1967 that when its dog handlers went on R&R, they would have the option of taking their dogs with them. During a news conference at the Da Nang Press Center, I asked LtGen Victor Krulak, Commanding General of all Marines in the Pacific, if the Marine Corps would adopt the Army policy. LtGen Krulak, nicknamed "The Brute" responded, "Sergeant Bowen, the Corps will not be giving its dogs time off for rest and relaxation."

My story on the Marine Corps going to the dogs was titled "Canine Scouts." It was the cover story for the July 1967 issue of *Leatherneck* Magazine.

CHAPTER 20

First 140mm Rockets Hit Da Nang

The guns and the bombs, the rockets and the
warships are all symbols of human failure.
~ Lyndon Baines Johnson,
36th President of the United States

Sunday, February 26, 1967, had been a lazy sort of day. Marines and correspondents at the CIB played a game of volleyball, wrote letters home, and generally goofed off. Gassaway, another correspondent, and I had played Scrabble and Pinochle for most of the afternoon and on into the evening. Gassaway and I were still at it at 3:10 a.m. when the first explosion shattered the quiet of the night. Then another—and another, followed by the sound of sirens. The explosions were coming from the direction of the Da Nang airfield. It was under attack.

I grabbed my camera, flak jacket, .45 caliber pistol and canteen—asked Gassaway for the keys to the AP jeep, and raced off into the night. I followed a fire truck going past the Press Center. It was on its way to the village of Ap Ba just outside the fence along the east side of the air base. Many of the shacks the Vietnamese called home were in flames.

In the beginning, I was the only American in the village. Rockets had also hit the air base and the American military were responding to the attack on their side of the fence. In about fifteen minutes, a U.S. Navy ambulance arrived—then some Air Force fire trucks. The village was still ablaze and the Air Force firemen and Vietnamese firefighters fought it with a vengeance. It was under control in a few hours.

I entered several tin and wood huts that had been severely damaged. In one of them, a young woman lay dead in her bed. In another, an old woman lay dead on the floor and two Vietnamese soldiers were removing her gold rings by candlelight.

Outside, U.S. Air Force firemen were busy fighting the fire and locating injured for transportation to the local hospital in a U.S. Navy ambulance. Several villagers lay dead on pieces of corrugated metal roofing. Another piece of tin held the limp bodies of two small children. The stench of burned wood and flesh filled the air.

Two children are laid out on corrugated metal roofing, all that remained of their home after rocket attack.

A few feet away, three young men were sifting through a pile of what appeared at first to be charcoal, but turned out to be the remains of a loved one who was cremated in the blistering fire. In the midst of all this tragedy, my camera found a small boy of about five years old, not understanding what had just occurred. He was grinning from ear to ear.

Village men sift through the ashes for bone fragments
of family members after rocket attack.

Young boy, uncomprehending of his surroundings,
smiles for the camera as boys are wont to do.

The elders stood or squatted and stared in disbelief. They had lived a relatively secure life in the shadow of the massive airfield, used by both U.S. and Vietnamese military and Vietnamese civilian aircraft. But, that was now a thing of the past. The war had visited them in the harshest way.

Old man watches his home and surrounding village
go up in flames following rocket attack on Da Nang.

The number of rockets fired in the wee hours of February 27 varied depending on who was keeping score. A survey of the launch site by Marines at first light revealed that one hundred twenty-six launching pads had been constructed. But, only sixty of them showed signs of being used.

Back home at the Press Center by the AP jeep following
my all-night coverage of the rocket attack.

A Russian made 140mm unguided rocket is four feet long. The warhead contains about ten pounds of high explosive. The fuse is fired on impact. The launch tube is aimed at the target and anchored to the ground. The rocket is inserted in the tube and launched electrically by an ordinary flash light battery. The Air Force said eighteen Russian-made 140mm rockets hit the airfield and fifty-six hit the adjacent village, a total of seventy-four. But, in the village, I made photos of what appeared to be mortar fragments. They did not look like rocket fragments.

The casualty figure was not disputed. Eleven airmen, including two security policemen, and one Marine were killed and thirty-five wounded on the airfield. Thirteen planes were damaged. Ap Ba village suffered a much greater loss—one hundred fifty homes were destroyed. Thirty-five villagers were killed and seventy were wounded.

Grieving mother squats in front of the body bag containing her child, killed during the rocket attack.

The rockets had been launched near the hamlet of Bo Ban (2) at the confluence of the Tuy Loan, Yen, and Cau Do Rivers about ten miles southwest of the airfield in the tactical area of responsibility of the 9th

Marine Regiment. Interrogation of a Vietcong who had surrendered to the South Vietnamese Army that day said the rockets were carried to the launch site by laborers and a unit of North Vietnamese soldiers the day before the attack. They came down out of the mountains with the rockets and launchers, put them in boats and ferried them to the launch site. The system was crude, but highly effective.

The area where the rockets were launched was known as Happy Valley. Elephant grass in the area grew as tall as ten feet, providing excellent cover and concealment for the enemy coming down out of the mountain. After that first 140mm rocket attack on Da Nang on February 27, 1967, Happy Valley acquired a new nickname—the Rocket Belt.

CHAPTER 21

Supply and Things That Go "Boom"

The problem of land mines is a global tragedy. In all
probability, land mines kill more children than soldiers,
and they keep killing after wars are over.
~ Bill Clinton, 42nd President of the United States

March was devoted to writing several stories for which I had already gathered information. I also found time to visit the FLC and "A" Company, 7th Engineers for two additional stories.

If you wore it, ate it, drove it, wrote with it, or made war with it, chances are it came from FLC—the Marine Corps' big supply house in Vietnam.

With two divisions, and part of a third in Vietnam—more than seventy thousand Marines—the standard practice of divisions requisitioning supplies from supply facilities in California, Georgia, or Philadelphia had become unruly.

The FLC was established to answer the problem. Torn clothing was mended at FLC's Textile Repair Section. The Bake Shop made enough bread to feed forty-two thousand Marines each day. Empty sand bags were in constant demand.

The FLC Bake Shop made enough bread
to feed 42,000 Marines each day.

FLC had more than sixty thousand items in stock and received about forty thousand requests for supply items each month. Enough of everything was kept on hand to last forty-five days.

Huge refrigerated buildings occupied one corner of the FLC compound. These were filled with meats, fresh vegetables, and fruit. A huge favorite of Marines in the field was recombined milk. Donuts and ice cream were also made by the Marine bakers and cooks at FLC.

Typewriters were constantly being repaired
because of the dust and grime.

There was a typewriter repair section, a motor vehicle repair section, and a section that traveled to Marine artillery bases throughout I Corps fixing malfunctioning artillery pieces. Each gun was overhauled every six months.

Vehicles received routine maintenance, including grease jobs when needed.

Each artillery gun in Vietnam was overhauled every six months.

Communications gear demanded a critical eye in Vietnam because of the weather conditions. Dust, mud, humidity, heat, rain, and cold would take turns knocking out the communication equipment. When a unit turned in a radio for repair, it was given a replacement on loan. Maintenance was performed as quickly as possible and the radio was usually back with its old outfit within the week.

Generators, designed primarily for use during the initial phase of an amphibious operation, caused the maintenance men a lot of headaches. They were used constantly because of the inadequate electrical power in Vietnam, and, as a result, they broke down frequently. Continuous maintenance was the only means currently available to combat the problem.

The mechanical brains of FLC was located in the IBM 360 computer building. That complex was capable of storing more than 64,000 bits of information. That would be considered minuscule in today's world where a 500 GB personal computer is capable of storing about 4.3 trillion bits of information. But, in 1967, it was a monumental achievement.

The mechanical brains of FLC was located
in the IBM 360 computer building.

My story on the FLC appeared in August. A few days after the magazine hit the stands, I receive a letter from Brigadier General J. E. Herbold, Jr., Commanding General of FLC,

> *Thank you for your very fine article on the Force Logistic Command in the August issue of Leatherneck. Your words and picture were most gratifying and were well received by FLC personnel.*

The engineers of "A" Company, 7th Engineers were responsible for clearing a four-mile stretch of Route 5, just outside their company compound, to Delta Company's combat base on Hill 41. It took about three hours to complete the daily "sweep" operation. It involved about a dozen Marines—six engineers, a fire team, and a few other grunts providing security.

Marines of "A" Company, 7th Engineers began each day sweeping Route 5 south of Da Nang for enemy mines and booby traps. Until their work was complete, nothing moved on the road and traffic built up behind them.

Three two-man mine detector teams were employed—one on each side of the road and one in the center. One engineer carried a mine detector. The second man was the "prober." When something was detected, the prober would gently insert his bayonet into the suspected spot in search of what caused the detector to "bleep."

The teams were staggered as they moved down the road. One side would move out first, followed by the team on the other side of the road. The team in the center would follow. A distance of twenty-five–fifty feet separated each team—front to back—just in case one of the teams set off a mine.

Marine probes with his bayonet
to safely remove the shoe mine.

Occasionally a shoe mine would be found and everything
halted until it was removed from the road.

Sergeant Philip Solomon said his company lost four trucks to mines on Route 5 during the first three months of 1967. He was determined to put a halt to those exploding mines. The Vietcong used all kinds of mines. Some of them were controlled remotely. Some were small boxes containing explosives. These were often buried in roads. They were designed to withstand the weight of a man. But, would detonate if a vehicle drove over it.

All culverts got the "once over."

Sgt Solomon should know. He was in the right seat of a six-by as it moved out down Route 5, southwest of Da Nang. The driver whistled softly as the big truck bounced along the unpaved road. A Marine riding in the back swore his teeth were being jarred loose.

Then, in the twitch of an eyelash, the carefree ride turned into a nightmare. Charlie had placed a mine in one of those holes he likes to dig.

"It was an electrical mine," Solomon recalled vividly, "but fortunately, the VC set it off too soon. It exploded just as the left front wheel began to pass over it."

Sgt Solomon had instinctively thrown his left arm in front of his face, and in doing so, caught some fragments in his forearm. His left leg was also hit.

"I died three times in those few seconds," Sgt Solomon said. The driver and the man riding in the back weren't injured. The Vietcong who set off the mine escaped in the confusion. Sgt Solomon was lucky someone else wasn't telling his story.

The Vietcong were experts at converting "duds," unexploded artillery shells or bombs, into mines. One of these "artillery dud" mines is particularly vivid in my memory, fifty years later. That incident was described in Chapter 18.

My story about the Marine engineers who put their lives on the line day in and day out searching for mines was published in the July issue along with the piece on Gen Greene's dogs.

CHAPTER 22

Back to the World—Again

It is not enough to be busy. So are the ants.
The question is: what are we busy about?
~ Henry David Thoreau

I packed and left Vietnam on April 2, 1967. My replacement was SSgt Bruce Martin, but he did not arrive until the end of April. The editors said I had written so many stories I had created a backlog. No sense adding to it, so SSgt Martin's visit was delayed a while. His wife didn't mind.

I arrived home on April 14. My wife was pregnant again, but there would be no announcement of the latest Bowen at the 5 O'clock Follies in Saigon. Our son, Bob, was born on May 29, 1967, at DeWitt Army Hospital at Fort Belvoir, Virginia. I was outside the nursery window with my camera when a nurse carried him out of the delivery room and placed him in his crib.

May 1967 was good to me. In addition to my third child, second son, I received several certificates for completing a variety of Marine Corps Institute courses and an honorable mention plaque for a photograph I had entered in the 1966 Military Photographer of the Year contest. The annual competition was sponsored by the Department of Defense, National Press Photographers Association, and the University of Missouri's School of Journalism. The plaque was a modest recognition of my work, but greatly appreciated. I also learned that month that I had made staff sergeant and would receive my "rocker" stripe on July 1. My new monthly salary would be three hundred thirty-five dollars and ten cents, plus housing and a clothing allowance.

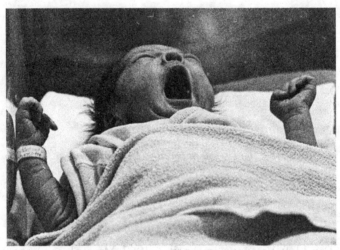

Son, Bob, arrived May 29, 1967.

One of several military course completion certificates received from *Leatherneck* Editor-Publisher Col Don Dickson, spring 1967.

Staff sergeant promotions have long-standing obligations.

That same month I received a letter from Jim Lucas, the Scripps Howard war correspondent in Vietnam, on Press Center stationery.

Too often in the rush of events, we neglect to tell a friend he has excelled.

I had dinner with General Walt last night. General Greene had called him from Washington a few minutes before he left his desk to tell him the Life magazine cover piece was on the stands and that it did him right proud.

I congratulated him.

"Thanks," he replied, "but none of them mean as much to me as that Leatherneck magazine piece by Sergeant Bowen."

Others agree, I recently visited one of our hospitals with our Three-Star Grunt. Every man seemed to have a copy of your April issue. At every bed, it was invariably: "Will you autograph this for me, Sir?"

To which I add my sincere concurrence and my heartfelt endorsement. It was superb, Bob, a job of which any writer could be proud. I was moved, as were many others.

We are all proud of you here.

Tom Bartlett, now a gunnery sergeant, had returned to *Leatherneck* Magazine following his two-semester course of photojournalism study at Syracuse University. He finished at the top of his class and was full of vim and vinegar. One day, when returning to the "writer's den" with a cup of hot coffee in each hand, I kicked on the door so someone would open it.

The door swung open and Gunny Bartlett was standing there with a pair of scissors in his hand and a mischievous grin on his face. Without batting an eye, he proceeded to cut my tie in half. I didn't have a spare tie, so I was forced to spend the remainder of the day with the bottom half of my tie held tightly in place with a paper clip beneath my regulation Marine Corps tie clasp. Gunny Bartlett had a footlocker full of practical jokes and you never knew what to expect from the funny gunny.

I returned to Camp Geiger in June, not for a refresher course in infantry training, but for a story on the way the course was being conducted based on the Vietnam experience. Chances were good the majority of Marines completing ITR that summer already had orders for Vietnam. How they applied themselves at Camp Geiger and what they learned would have a big bearing on whether they survived their first tour of combat duty.

Camp Geiger logo.

Camp Geiger is located at Camp Lejeune on the coast of North Carolina. The base was established in 1941 to practice and develop amphibious landing techniques for World War II. Camp Geiger was known as Tent City then. The amphibious landings rehearsed at Tent City's Onslow Beach proved to be effective at Guadalcanal and other islands in the Pacific theater.

The Corps trained fifty-seven thousand Marines at Camp Geiger in 1966. Among other supply items used for this training were twenty-seven million rounds of small arms ammunition, seventy-seven 3.5-inch rockets, and eighty-five thousand hand grenades.

You can't skimp when it comes to training young men—and in today's climate—women for combat. In 1967, a sign over the door of the S-3 Training office at Camp Geiger read: "Let no man's ghost say your training let him down." My story on Camp Geiger appeared in the August issue.

On June 19, Gunny Head and I flew commercially to Montreal, Canada, to do a story on the Marine detachment assigned as security for the U.S. Pavilion at the Canadian World Exposition 1967. Each of the thirty-eight Marines were chosen because they had served in Vietnam. Instead of jungle utilities, they wore dress blues with anodized medals. A most impressive sight.

A Marine was posted at ten different areas of the U.S. Pavilion during the twelve operating hours each day. Each Marine stood a six-hour shift. They had no weapons, only a smile and a snappy salute for all who ventured to stop and ask a question.

U.S. Geodic Dome Pavilion at Expo '67.

While in Montreal, Gunny Head and I were the guests of the Canadian Army and stayed at the Montreal Garrison. Our nine-page report on the Expo duty, complete with fifteen photos plus the cover, appeared in the September 1967 issue of *Leatherneck* Magazine.

Overlooking site of 1967 Expo in Montreal.

CHAPTER 23

Syracuse University

I think everyone should go to college and get a degree
and then spend six months as a bartender and six months
as a cabdriver. Then they would really be educated.
~ Al McGuire, Collegiate Basketball Coach

The Bowen family packed up and headed for Syracuse University on August 18, 1967, arriving there—following a little vacation time in Norfolk—on September 1. The graduate-level course in photojournalism included classes in journalism, reporting, news magazine photography, publications photography, public speaking, magazine reporting, graphics design, human group behavior, color photography, and several other photography classes. The class included thirteen sailors and me—the lone Marine.

The Navy Program in Photojournalism was designed by Syracuse Professor Fred Demarest in 1963. Each class included at least one Marine. Mine was the fifth class.

I would not hazard a guess as to how many rolls of film I used between September 1967 and May 1968, but it would fill more than one bread box. We had specific assignments, but we were expected to hone our photographic eye at every opportunity. So, when not in class or on an assignment, I could be found roaming around the zoo, at one of several cemeteries in the city, at university athletic events, fire stations, construction sites, lectures, or simply roaming the campus and city's streets making pictures.

Professor Fred Demarest, founder of the
Syracuse Navy Program in Photojournalism.

Ringling Brothers Circus clown caught my attention.

When the Ringling Brothers Circus came to town, I was there. When demonstrations were held on campus to protest against Dow Chemical for inventing the Agent Orange defoliant used in Vietnam, I was there with my camera. When renown portrait photographer Yousuf Karsh visited the university, I made his informal portrait. I processed and printed it quickly, mounted it, and before he left that afternoon, he autographed it for me.

Renowned photographer Yosuf Karsh gave us his
insight of the work that lay ahead for us.

With three children to make happy when Christmas arrived, I
took a part-time job as a customer services representative at the local
K-Mart. As students, we were not heavily committed over the holidays
and the extra money sure came in handy.

Early in the second semester, we boarded a bus for a ninety-mile
trip to George Eastman House in Rochester and the Kodak factory
there. Kodak produced our film, chemicals, and photographic paper.
The one-day field day was a welcome break in our photojournalism
curriculum, but most of us couldn't resist bringing our camera with us
to document what we saw. So much for a break in the routine.

One of my first "free time" visits was to the Syracuse *Herald-
American* office to offer my services as a freelance photojournalist. To
sweeten the pot, I offered whatever story I might produce at no cost.
It was a win-win. Anything I had published would result in extra credit
at the university. The newspaper would get free help.

When I left *Leatherneck* Magazine I had arranged to write seven
monthly features titled "Portrait of the Enemy" and I was receiving
fifty dollars for each feature. So, all of my writing and photographic
efforts at Syracuse were not going unpaid.

One five-page photo spread in the Sunday *Empire* Magazine was titled "The Many Faces of Vietnam Kids." It featured photos I had made of Vietnamese children in 1966 and 1967. Another Empire photo story showed my son, Jack, as a "make believe" photographer going through all the steps to make, process, and print a photograph of his sister, Donna. That photo story earned me an unsolicited and unexpected twenty-five dollar check. For straight news writing, the newspaper published reports I wrote on a city government proposal to extend the school year, and one on the city parks gearing up to open after the long winter.

Son, Jack, selects a photo to print for a newspaper
feature titled "My Son the Photographer."

The 1967 Silver Anchor Awards were announced in December and I won six certificates of achievement for my *Leatherneck* Magazine features and a Weston light meter for my photographs. The annual competition was sponsored by the Armed Forces Writers League.

Daughter, Donna, listens intently as Dad tells her
how to remove her cupcakes from the oven.

The winter of 1967–1968 was bitter cold in upstate New York. Eighty-one cumulative inches of snow fell and temperatures were frequently below 20 degrees Fahrenheit. Winters in upstate New York traditionally produce what the natives call a "dry cold" meaning that even with subfreezing temperatures you can often go outside without a coat. That did not mean the hairs in your nose would not freeze, which is something I vividly remember happening to me many times.

The freezing temperature was also hard on our cameras. We were issued the Topcon Super D, an excellent 35mm single lens reflex camera. Like most mechanical equipment that relies on lubrication for its moving parts, the camera had a tendency to lock up in subfreezing weather. I found this to be the case when I drove to Lake Oneida one weekend to photograph some dog sled races.

Gen Greene served as Commandant of the Marine Corps from 1964 through 1967, the buildup years for the war in Vietnam. In January 1968, our news instructor gave us an assignment to interview someone on a subject that was currently in the news. Vietnam and the draft were big topics at the time. The Marine Corps prided itself on not having to draft, but with the ever-increasing demands brought on by the war in Vietnam, the Corps had to put its pride aside and take men through the draft.

With Gen Greene being so heavily involved in the buildup, I called some friends in Washington, D.C., obtained Gen Greene's home phone number, and called him to learn his thoughts on the subject. The general remembered me from *Leatherneck* Magazine and was gracious in his willingness to discuss the Corps and the draft.

Gen Greene believed that taking part in the draft was giving the Marine Corps a caliber of men they did not normally see in the recruiters' office. These draftees were, for the most part, college graduates. They were highly intelligent, easily trained, and a cut above the average high school graduate. I got an A on the assignment with a "plus" added for having the gall to call a retired four-star general at home on a Sunday afternoon during the closing weeks of the professional football season.

Back in the day, each photojournalism class was assigned a class project that used photos made by members of the class during the two semesters they were at Syracuse. Our project was the students, staff, and faculty. We titled our booklet "These People." I was the editor and I selected at least one photo from each classmate for the publication.

In March, I was notified that I had won Runner-Up honors in the 1967 Military Photographer of the Year competition. Individual awards won included honorable mention and "in show" in the News category, a second place and third place in the Portrait category, and first place in Picture Story.

My awards in the Military Photographer of the Year Competition resulted in a cover feature in the monthly magazine *Government Photography*, titled "The Agony of War," the nine-page feature included twelve of my combat photos from Vietnam, including the cover. I also had a "one man" show of my Vietnam combat photos in the lobby of the Newhouse Communication Center. I titled the show "My War."

On March 29, 1968, I received orders that read: ". . . upon completion of the photojournalism course about June 1," I was to proceed by July 11 and report to Marine Corps Base, Camp Pendleton, California, for temporary processing and further transportation as an August 1968 replacement for duty with West Pacific ground forces. I was going back to Vietnam.

I graduated at the top of my class. It was the third straight year a former *Leatherneck* Magazine staffer had earned those honors, Gunny Berger in 1966, Gunny Bartlett in 1967, and now me in 1968. I earned nine As, two Bs, and thirty-one college credits.

While at Syracuse, I fabricated a darkroom in the basement of the house I rented in Mattydale, a suburb of Syracuse. I used cardboard from the boxes containing my personal belongings when we moved. So, anytime I needed to process my film and make prints, I had a place to get the job done.

My closest friend in the class, Rich Pendergist, a Navy petty officer second class, and I were always out on self-generated shooting assignments. A favorite location was the small town of Tully, south of Syracuse. One of our classmates, Jack Gravat, rented there. PO2 Pendergist and I spent several of our final weekends in Tully making photos at the Tully Barn. This was an old barn on the town's main street that doubled as a restaurant during the week and a bar and dance hall on Friday and Saturday nights—complete with country band. The owner was the leader of the band. When PO2 Pendergist and I were there, I was always invited to join in with my "spoons"— especially when the song was "Rocky Top."

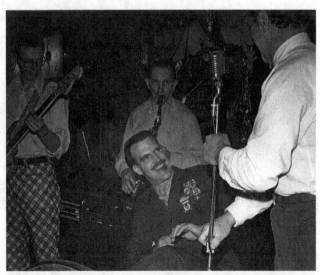

Playing the spoons at The Barn in Tully, New York.

I left Syracuse on June 13. Adams had been awarded the Pulitzer Prize for his photo of a South Vietnamese general executing a Vietcong in Saigon during Tet of that year. On the drive home to Norfolk, Virginia, I stopped in Bogota, New Jersey, to congratulate Adams on his recognition. The AP had produced an 8x10 announcement glossy containing an image of Eddie and his award-winning photograph for release over the wire. Eddie gave me a copy of that photo. He autographed it, "'To Bob, the new Corps and a good guy.'-Eddie Adams." It has a place of honor on my "man cave" wall.

CHAPTER 24

1st Marine Division, Vietnam

If I had one more division like this First Marine
Division I could win this war.
~ General Douglas McArthur, General of the Armies, Korea

I was anxious to get back to Vietnam. Some of the heaviest fighting of the war had taken placed earlier that year and I wanted to get back into action before the war ended.

The fighting in 1968 began in earnest on January 30, the first day of the Tet Lunar New Year celebrations. In the past, there had been agreements to cease-fire during Tet. When North and South Vietnam announced on national radio broadcasts that there would be a two-day cease-fire during the holiday it did not come as a surprise and both sides breathed a collective sigh of relief. On January 30, the Communists launched their attack. It began during the early morning hours on the first day of Tet. In Vietnamese, the offensive that year was commonly called *Tết Mậu Thân* (Tet, year of the monkey). South Vietnamese military planners called it the "General Offensive and Uprising" (*Cuộc Tổng tiến công và nổi dậy*). In American military circles countrywide fighting was referred to as the "Tet Offensive."

The attacks were launched throughout South Vietnam. More than eighty thousand Communist troops struck more than one hundred towns and cities, including thirty-six provincial capitals, five autonomous cities, seventy-two district towns, and the southern capital,

Saigon. The offensive was the largest military operation conducted by either side up to that time.

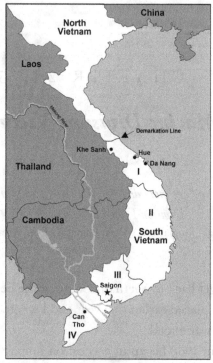

Vietnam
Courtesy of Robin Kern

The attacks stunned the U.S. and South Vietnamese Armies, causing them to temporarily lose control of several cities. They quickly regrouped to beat back the attacks, inflicting massive casualties on the Communist forces. During the Battle of Hue, intense fighting lasted for a month resulting in the destruction of the city by the Americans while the Communists executed thousands of residents. More than five thousand North Vietnamese and Vietcong fighters were killed during the Battle of Hue. The U.S. lost one hundred forty-two men.

Fighting continued for two months around the Marine Corps' combat base at Khe Sahn. Although both sides claimed victory, the offensive was a military defeat for the Communists.

The actual number of NVA and Vietcong killed in the fighting is unknown, but more than sixteen hundred enemy bodies were counted and more than fifty-five hundred were believed to have been killed. American Marines lost two hundred seventy-four men killed and two thousand, five hundred forty-one wounded. The Tet Offensive had a profound effect on the U.S. government and shocked the American public, which had been led to believe that the Communists could not mount such a massive effort.

With that backdrop, I reported in at Camp Pendleton, California, at 10:15 p.m. on July 12. An eleven-day Combat Correspondent Course awaited. The course was conducted by an old friend, Gunny Chris Evans, the man I replaced as editor of the "Sound Off" column when I first joined *Leatherneck* Magazine in 1964. Having served as a combat correspondent in Vietnam in 1966 and 1967, I spent most of my time helping Gunny Evans instruct the students with no Vietnam experience.

We left Camp Pendleton by bus, bound for Travis Air Force Base, north of San Francisco, on August 5. There were a total of fifty-seven Marines on the flight, a mix of enlisted and officers. They included one other staff sergeant writer, Brian Finlayson; two gunnery sergeants, Don Coleman and E. J. Moore, and a photographer, Staff Sergeant D. D. Allen.

In its historical series of booklets about the Vietnam War, the Marine Corps describes 1968 as "The Defining Year." And, having missed the action of the first six months, the Tet Offensive, and the Marine Corps battles at Khe Sahn and Hue, I was anxious to get started covering the second half. I didn't have long to wait.

I arrived in Vietnam on August 12. I checked in at Headquarters Company, Headquarters Battalion, First Marine Division on Hill 327 at 8:30 a.m. and was assigned to the Division Informational Services Office.

Captain Mordecai "Mawk" Arnold was the Informational Services Officer. He arranged for the Division Photo Lab to issue me a Nikon camera and a steady supply of black & white film. He also let me use his personal photo lab he had set up in the ISO Quonset hut. Then he cut me loose to roam throughout the Division to cover the war.

Capt Mordecai "Mawk" Arnold.

It was an election year and we had our share of politicians "dropping by" for a visit. General Curtis LeMay, vice presidential candidate visited, as did Barry Goldwater, and a host of lesser dignitaries. We even had our own Marine with political connections in the person of Chuck Robb, President Johnson's son-in-law. I covered Robb's promotion to major shortly after arriving in country. I treasured the promotion cigar he provided after donning the gold maple leaves of a major, as I did the cigar he gave me a short while later to announce the birth of his first daughter, Lucy.

MajGen Carl Youngdale, CG of the 1st MarDiv, pins
on the insignia of newly promoted Maj Chuck Robb.

Major General Carl A. Youngdale, commanding general of the Division, was earning his two-star salary when I arrived in country. You could almost smell another enemy offensive in the air. And, MajGen Youngdale had predicted as much in his daily reports to Lieutenant General Robert Cushman, commanding general of III MAF.

The Cam Le Bridge spanning the Song Cau Do River heading south out of Da Nang on Route One, was the scene of some very heavy fighting on August 23, 1968, shortly after I arrived. Captain Bill Moore was the commander of Alpha Company, 1st Battalion, 27th Marine Regiment. His company helped turn the tide and prevented the NVA from capturing the bridge.

Cam Le Bridge, south of Da Nang.
Scene of heavy fighting, August 23, 1968.

After the battle, one hundred fifty NVA soldiers of the V-25 battalion were killed in a two-day pitched battle in the hamlet of Qua Giang (2) a few miles south of the bridge. The old men and women of the hamlet buried the bodies in a mass grave. The sign hastily hung in the hamlet read: "The communist regime is the most brutal regime."

Hamlet elders in Qua Giang (2) remove dead NVA soldiers
after a failed attack following the fighting at Cam Le Bridge.

Mawk's Snuffies were in full swing during my time with the First
Marine Division. Led by Sgt Dale Dye, the Snuffies were a group of
irreverent but talented young Marine writers and broadcasters who
helped put a face on the Vietnam War with their dispatches about the
grunts in the bush and paddies.

Snuffies of First Marine Division ISO, 1968.
Top Row (l-r): Rick Lavers, Jim Hardy, Woodrow Cheeley,
Jeff Ault, Tim Godfrey, Jerry Goodall, LCpl Kerry Dale Hunter.
Bottom Row (l-r): Art Kybat, Eric Grimm, Bob Rea, Frank Wiley,
Sgt Dale Dye, Sgt Bob Bayer. Venue was the Snuffie Bar
in Hooch 13. Occasion was grand opening of the bar
which required civilian clothes for attendance.

Dale Dye retired a limited duty officer (LDO) captain and forged a second career as a military advisor and actor in such movies as *Platoon*, *Saving Private Ryan*, and *Band of Brothers* to name a few.

I covered portions of ten named operations while with the First Marine Division: Allen Brook, Mameluke Thrust, Dodge Valley, Talledaga Canyon, Maui Peak, Henderson Hill, Garrard Bay, Meade River, Taylor Common, and Sussex Bay. Photos made were released to the news media by the Marine Corps CIB. My reports were published primarily by the Marines' Vietnam weekly *Sea Tiger.*

I accompanied 1/1, commanded by Captain Hank Trautwein, on Operation Maui Peak in early October 1968. Our objective was Hill 604, some twenty-five miles southwest of Da Nang—part of the infamous Charlie Ridge. The climb was practically straight up. Along the way we faced mountain streams and triple canopy and relied heavily on vines and small bushes to pull ourselves to the top. We saw no enemy action the first day, but the sound of gunfire from other units engaged with the NVA reverberated through the mountains. Twenty-eight Marines were killed during the nineteen-day operation. The enemy lost two hundred two killed.

Center: Capt Hank Trautwein commanding officer of C 1/1, briefs his men at the start of Operation Maui Peak.

I did my best to keep up with the much younger Snuffies until a bout with sinusitis forced my medical evacuation to Guam for an operation in early January 1969.

Before my medical problems arose, Capt Arnold had pulled me

aside and suggested I apply for the warrant officer program. He wrote a great recommendation, as did Lieutenant Colonel Alphonse A. Laporte, commanding officer of 1/1.

LtCol A. A. Laporte, commanding officer of 1/1.

La Porte's letter read, in part:

> *As the Commanding Officer of the 1st Battalion, 1st Marines it was my privilege to know SSgt Bob Bowen as a combat Marine. The troopers, Staff NCO's and officers welcomed him wherever he went. By his example, he spurred on my Marines to probe harder, deeper and better our search and clear operations; much of the enemy ordnance and food supplies which we found on these operations can be attributed to the high interest he generated by his own search efforts.*
>
> *I would welcome SSgt Bowen on any mission assigned to my battalion and would gladly accept him in an "0369" billet, confident he would perform admirably as a Company Gunnery Sergeant or Platoon Leader. He is in every respect a professional*

Marine, accomplishing his mission in keeping with the highest
traditions of the Marine Corps and the Naval Service.

Nothing to do at that point but sit back and await the selection board's report. And that would not come until the following year.

Meade River was the largest Marine helicopter borne operation of the war. I was designated media coordinator for the operation meaning I was charged with keeping the civilian correspondents briefed each day, assisting them with their coverage, and arranging for briefings by the officers directing the operation. But, I did manage to get out and cover some of the fighting up close and personal.

Meade River claimed the lives of one hundred eight Marines from the seven battalions taking part in the twenty-nine-day operation. The enemy lost one thousand twenty-three killed and one hundred twenty three captured.

CH-46 helicopter disgorges its load of combat Marines
during Operation Meade River.

Marines of B Company, 1/1, had an unusual part time assignment for grunts. They had a small fleet of Boston whalers, called skimmers, they used to patrol the rivers south of Da Nang. These small boats, powered by a Mercury outboard motor, were the ideal transportation for inserting small patrols, retrieving patrols, wounded Marines, and captured enemy soldiers. I accompanied them on two occasions in October 1968.

Marines of B 1/1 escort a pair of captured Vietcong in their "skimmer" on the Song Cau Do River south of Da Nang.

I was awarded the Navy Commendation Medal with Combat V for my work with the First Marine Division. I also received the Purple Heart Medal after stepping into a cleverly disguised hole on a trail bordering a rice paddy and impaling my shin on a punji stake.

Shortly before Christmas, my nose began bleeding profusely. I'd wake up in the middle of the night and my pillow would be drenched in blood. A few trips to sick day and it was determined I had sinusitis. While awaiting medevac to Guam for an operation I was awakened one night in my tent by the sound of a .45 pistol shot.

The following morning, I discovered the origin of the pistol shot. A visiting master sergeant from Okinawa had shot himself. He had come to Vietnam to take advantage of a tax-free reenlistment bonus but after getting paid, he promptly lost all of his money in a poker game.

He was no better at shooting himself than he was at playing poker and while he did lose one eye, he lived. When I arrived at the Naval Hospital on Guam, he was there telling everyone how he had been shot in an ambush.

While recuperating from the sinus operation at the Portsmouth Naval Hospital, Portsmouth, Virginia, I received orders to return to *Leatherneck* Magazine.

CHAPTER 25

Back to Leatherneck Magazine

Why in hell can't the Army do it if the Marines can?
They are the same kind of men;
why can't they be like Marines?
~ General John J. "Black Jack" Pershing

Shortly after arriving back at the magazine I learned of an unusual assignment some AmTrac Marines from Camp Lejeune, Jacksonville, North Carolina, had received. So, in May 1969, I was at the Kennedy Space Center, Cape Canaveral (Titusville), Florida, for the launch of Apollo 10, the final Apollo mission space flight before man's first attempt to land and walk on the moon.

Thirteen Marines from Camp Lejeune pose for a group photo in front of their specially configured AmTracs prior to the launch of Apollo 10.

The Marines were there with two specially configured amphibious tractors designed to retrieve the Apollo capsule should the launch be aborted within the first few seconds. Everything went as planned—less the recovery effort—and my story was the cover piece for the August *Leatherneck* Magazine, one month after Apollo 11 and the first moon walk.

Marines stand on top of their AmTrac as Apollo 10 blasts off from the Kennedy Space Center in May 1969. Two months later, the first man to walk on the moon landed in Apollo 11.

From Cape Canaveral, I drove south to Key West to accompany Marines of the 2nd Force Reconnaissance Battalion on some Lockout training. It involved leaving a submerged submarine through a torpedo hatch while the submarine was underway.

On the way to Key West, I made an overnight stop in Miami to visit Bob Gassaway, the AP correspondent I had met in Vietnam two years earlier. Gassaway was the AP correspondent assigned to Miami in 1969. We went to a movie that night to see the Italian crime film, *The Vatican Affair*, starring Walter Pidgeon.

The Lockout training was a tremendous experience. We had rubber boat training one night with a rather lengthy swim back to the beach after we reached our destination. The swim back was a fast one after a school of barracuda crossed our path. Not to mention the jellyfish that hindered our swim. Onboard the USS *Sealion* (APSS-315), the Marines awaited their turn to enter the trunk. The dives off the coast began at a depth of twenty feet and graduated to about thirty-five feet before the men began working with the submarine. Each depth was tackled four to six times, after which the Marines swam some fifteen hundred yards to shore.

Reconnaissance Marines take part in rubber boat exercise prior to boarding submarine for Lockout training at Key West, Florida, 1969.

The submarine used for the training, the USS *Sealion*, was one of two U.S. submarines assigned the mission of carrying assault troops to hostile shores.

In World War II, she participated in six war patrols, earning five battle stars on the Pacific Area Service Medal and the Presidential Unit Citation for sinking eight merchant ships and three warships. One of these was the *Kongo*, the only Japanese battleship sunk by a submarine during the war.

The *Sealion* was decommissioned after the war, but in 1948 she was converted into a troop carrier and put back on active duty. She could carry detachments of about one hundred troops, complete with equipment.

Once inside the submarine, a Navy Corpsman was in charge. Orders were sent via radio and the Marines repeated each one before carrying out the assigned task.

Vents were opened, water was allowed to fill the trunk to a certain level, a hatch was opened, and on a signal from the trunk operator, the divers exited the trunk, one at a time. After blowing all his air and getting the second thumbs-up from the safety diver, the Marine headed for the surface.

As each man bobbed to the surface, a Navy doctor was standing by in a rubber boat to ask if he was okay. After the affirmative reply, the divers swam to the side of another rubber boat and awaited their turn to reenter the submarine.

Everything worked in reverse when entering the submerged submarine. The divers reached the submarine by pulling themselves down a rope. As the lead swimmer entered the trunk he sounded off, "first swimmer in." This was continued until the four men were back inside the trunk.

The hatch was then closed (dogged), the vent was opened and the water was forced out of the trunk by air. A second hatch was opened and the men left the trunk and climbed down a ladder into the belly of the submarine.

As soon as the last man stepped off the ladder another team entered the trunk and the cycle began again. The Marines left the submarine during the day and night, while she was under way. It was a learning experience I never hoped to have to use but training I needed to understand what the Marines had just gone through. I was quick to decline an offer to join the platoon for parachute training scheduled for the following month at Fort Benning, Georgia.

My report on the AmTrac Marines at Kennedy Space Center was the cover story for the August issue of *Leatherneck* Magazine. The Lockout piece was the cover article for the September issue.

I was still peeling skin off my back from a severe sunburn I acquired at Key West when I headed back to Vietnam for my fourth tour as a combat correspondent. This trip was planned to last six months. It was to include the usual combat operations, the withdrawal of the 9th

Marines after four years in country, and to accompany a few Marines on R&R to Christchurch, New Zealand, followed by a hop to Antarctica for a story on a handful of Marines assigned to the annual Operation Deep Freeze scientific venture.

The final phase of my planned trip never got off the ground. I was with a company of Marines on a search and destroy mission, part of Operation Pipestone Canyon IV on Go Noi Island, south of Da Nang when Astronaut Neal Armstrong stepped on the moon. One Marine was overheard commenting to a buddy, "Now, there's a difference in education for you. Those two guys just walked on the moon and we're going to take a walk in the sun."

Almost every Marine had a small portable radio plugged into his ear when Armstrong uttered the now famous "That's one small step for a man, one giant leap for mankind."

Later, President Richard Nixon spoke by telephone to Armstrong. MSgt Allen commented, "I can't get in touch with "A" Company a mile down the road and the president can talk to the man on the moon."

MSgt Edison Allen—Operation Pipestone Canyon IV, July 1969.

Before we left the field, word arrived that I had been selected for gunny and the Warrant Officer Program. I would have to end my assignment to Vietnam sooner than I had planned. There was still time for some more stories about Marines in Vietnam before I left. I titled my final walk in the sun article, "Two Walks."

I traveled north to Vandegrift Combat Base in Quang Tri Province to gather photos and information for an article about the 9th Marines leaving Vietnam after almost four continuous years in combat. The regiment had landed at Red Beach on March 8, 1965. They left Vietnam in increments. The 1st Battalion pulled out first, followed by the 2nd and 3rd Battalions. The men were flown to Da Nang in C-130 transport planes and trucked to the Navy's deep water pier at the base of Monkey mountain where ceremonies were held before boarding the USS *Paul Revere* for the voyage to Okinawa.

The 9th Marines removed all of the ammunition from the weapons and magazines prior to boarding the USS *Paul Revere*, bound for Okinawa and further duty at Camp Schwab.

Utah Mesa, a joint U.S. Marine, U.S. Army, and South Vietnamese Army operation, was in its fourth day when a rumor that the 9th Marine Regiment was leaving Vietnam began stirring up interest in Alpha Company, 1/9. President Nixon had announced he would be withdrawing twenty-five thousand troops from Vietnam that year and the 9th Marines had drawn a short straw. Even as the rumor became known to be reality, the Marines fought on. Utah Mesa, began on June 12 to clear the enemy from the vicinity of Khe Sahn, site of fierce fighting the previous year. It ended on July 9.

During the Vietnam War, 1/9 earned the dubious nickname "The Walking Dead." It sustained the highest casualty rate of any Marine battalion, 93.63 percent, based on an authorized strength of eight hundred. It was in combat for forty-seven months and seven days and suffered seven hundred forty-seven killed during that time.

Men of the 1/9, the "Walking Dead" wrap up Operation Utah
and prepare to leave Vietnam after four years.

When Utah Mesa came to a halt, the Marines returned to Vandegrift Combat Base. They had left three hundred and nine enemy dead on the battlefield. During their last few days there before leaving for Okinawa, the enemy made life miserable for the Marines. For two days in a row the NVA peppered the camp with rockets. The Marines were forced to think more about leaving Vietnam alive than just leaving Vietnam.

While the 9th Marines were sailing to Okinawa, I boarded a C-130 cargo plane in Da Nang and flew there. I wanted to be on hand to photograph their arrival. When they debarked at White Beach, they boarded cattle cars and were taken to Camp Schwab. Two stories, "The Ninth Moves Out" and "The Ninth Moves In," appeared in the November 1969 issue of the *Leatherneck* Magazine.

Also in July 1969, Marine helicopter squadron HMM-165 and fighter squadron VMFA-334 left Vietnam. The Black Knights of 165 arrived in Vietnam in October 1966. The squadron participated in every Allied operation in northern I Corps from time of arrival until they pulled out three years later. Everything from medical evacuations to resupply, troop lifts, and reconnaissance insertions and extractions—"165" had seen them all. It was time to take a rest.

The Falcons of 334 arrived in 1968, but in one year of combat operations, the squadron of F-4J Phantoms flew more than sixty-four hundred combat sorties, compiled more than seventy-three hundred flight hours and dropped twelve thousand, five hundred tons of bombs on enemy positions and infiltration routes. My report on both squadrons' departure appeared in the October 1969 *Leatherneck* Magazine issue along with a story on Reconnaissance Marines on Hill 200, southwest of Da Nang.

Hill 200 rises close to the edge of the mountain range and gave Marines of B Company, 1st Reconnaissance Battalion a good view of known enemy sanctuaries, such as the Arizona Area and the notorious Charlie Ridge. The men kept a constant 360-degree watch for signs of enemy activity in both areas remote from the hill, and avenues of approach to the hill. It's dull and it's tedious, but their efforts paid off many times.

Marines of B Company, 1st Reconnaissance Battalion had a good view of known enemy sanctuaries from their perch atop Hill 200 near Charlie Ridge. They cheer as an OV-10 Bronco flies overhead.

In addition to the platoon of reconnaissance Marines, a two-man artillery forward observation team made its home on the hill. The team was on loan to 1st Reconnaissance from the 11th Marine Artillery Regiment at An Hoa and its members often spent more than a month on the hill before being relieved. I spent two days on the Hill, got my story and returned to the Press Center to write and prepare for more adventures.

One of those adventures was a flight out of Da Nang with an Air Force AC-47 "Spooky" gunship.

We'd been circling Da Nang at four thousand feet, drilling holes in the sky, when the radio crackled.

"Spooky One-One . . . Spooky One-One. This is Four-One India . . . over."

The drilling operation ceased immediately.

"Four-One India, this is Spooky One-One. What can we do for ya, podner?"

And so it began. A unit on the ground was in contact with the enemy south of Hoi An and the forward air observer with the unit had requested an Air Force AC-47 "Spooky" gunship. Flares lit up the area and bullets from the aircraft's three mini-guns, each loaded with two thousand rounds of 7.62mm ammunition blasted the assigned target.

Baaaaaarup!

A ball of fire erupted from the six-barreled mini-gun and a steady stream of red hot dots and dashes streaked to the target. The stench of burned gunpowder filled the air.

"We're gonna have to leave ya, podner," the pilot radioed to the Marines on the ground. "We've drawn another mission."

"Hate to see you go. Like to thank you for the help."

"That's okay, podner. Any time."

"We'll try and get you some KBA [kills by air] in the morning," the platoon radioman said after three more "thank yous."

And that's the way it was when you were a member of "A" Detachment, 4th Special Operations Squadron, based at Da Nang. Flying was done only during the hours of darkness and you were on duty twelve hours a day. Your nightly runs were scheduled for five hours, and you were known to land and reload four times during that period.

You flew in support of any ground unit in I Corps that needed you. You showed no favoritism in your work. Captured enemy weapons hung on the wall of your ready room attested to the gratefulness of Marine, Army, Korean, and South Vietnamese units.

"Spooky," along with reports of a rocket attack on Da Nang in September, "Too Quiet, Too Long," and a report on a children's hospital established by the 3rd Marine Division in Quang Tri Province, "Hope for Tomorrow," appeared in the December 1969 issue of *Leatherneck* Magazine.

I left for home after covering one more operation in September.

Barrier Island had been on the list of recommended places for enemy soldiers to take off their packs and enjoy a few days away from the war. But, that was before troops of the 2nd Korean Marine Corps Brigade stormed ashore in a helicopter and waterborne assault and put an end to the fun and games.

Located on the coast of the East China Sea, about twenty miles south of Da Nang, Barrier Island had long been a favorite Vietcong and NVA sanctuary. Communist soldiers, beaten back during encounters with Allied units in the Dodge City/Go Noi Island area and in the mountains south of there, would often retreat to the relative security of Barrier Island.

Supplies were hoarded there, small hospitals were set up in dank underground bunkers, and the absence of day-to-day Allied activity on the island made it an ideal spot for the enemy to regroup, lick his wounds, and plan future offensives.

On September 6, rockets slammed into Da Nang, killing and wounding military and civilian alike. It was 1:55 a.m. when the first rounds whistled overhead on their way to unsuspecting targets throughout the city.

One 122mm rocket slammed into a Butler building containing "dry" provisions at the Naval Support Activity's covered storage area.

No one was injured and the cleanup crew managed a few lighthearted comments. "We're making macaroni tonight," one officer said.

Correspondent Esper wrote about the attack in his daily coverage of the war for the AP. His dispatch reached the *Ledger-Star* newspaper in my hometown.

"Associated Press photographer Hugh Van Es and a Marine combat correspondent, Staff Sgt. Bob Bowen, USMC, of Norfolk, Virginia, were in the Da Nang area when the barrage hit," Esper wrote. "Bowen was blown off his feet but suffered only a skinned knee."

The following day, Republic of Korea Marines launched Operation Victory Dragon 15-1. It was the Koreans first amphibious landing ever. U.S. Marines of the 1st Battalion, 26th Marine Regiment, landed first and established a block to the south of the operational area. The Marines called the operation Defiant Stand.

South Korean Marine takes up a firing position in a hedgerow
surrounded by cactus on Barrier Island during
Operation Defiant Stand, September 1969.

During the twelve-day operation south of Chu Lai, the Allies killed two hundred ninety-three enemy soldiers, captured six and many of his weapons (both individual and crew-served), destroyed his underground hideouts, smashed the Vietcong infrastructure there, and freed the innocent Vietnamese fishermen and farmers from the yoke of Communist taxation and threat of terrorism. The Americans lost five Marines killed and thirty-nine wounded. One Republic of Korea Marine was killed and five wounded.

Republic of Korea Marines of the Blue Dragon Brigade escort a Vietcong suspect as he points out some concealed hiding places of the enemy.

It was time for me to take off my pack, write one final Vietnam War story, and head for home. My war was over. What had begun in January 1966 had spanned about twenty months of in-country combat operations in 1966, 1967, 1968, and 1969. There had been countless patrols, rocket attacks, lonely outposts, hospital visits, flights in every imaginable kind of aircraft, and walks in the sun.

I had covered twenty-one major named operations and countless lesser patrols, ambushes, village sweeps, county fairs, medcaps, and other civic affairs programs. In 1966 there were Operations Big Lodge, Double Eagle, Double Eagle II, New York, and Utah.

In 1967 I covered Operations Tuscaloosa, Independence, and Stone. My busiest year was 1968, when I was a member of the First Marine Division. That year, I covered Operations Allen Brook, Mameluke Thrust, Dodge Valley, Talladega Canyon, Maui Peak, Henderson Hill, Garrad Bay, Meade River, Taylor Common, and Sussex Bay.

I closed out my coverage of the war in 1969 with Operations Pipestone Canyon IV, Utah Mesa, and Defiant Stand. The report on my final combat operation titled "Barrier Island" appeared in the January 1970 issue of *Leatherneck* Magazine.

My war came to an end following Operation Defiant Stand, 1969. I had covered twenty-one major named operations and countless lesser patrols, ambushes, village sweeps, county fairs, and an assortment of civic affairs programs.

CHAPTER 26

Warrant Office Screening and The Basic School

Marines I see as two breeds, Rottweilers or Dobermans, because
Marines come in two varieties, big and mean, or skinny and mean.
They're aggressive on the attack and tenacious on defense.
They've got really short hair and they always go for the throat.
~ Rear Admiral "Jay" R. Stark

Back in the world, as we called the States after serving in Vietnam, was a totally new experience. In Vietnam, young Marines wore jungle utilities, flak jackets, steel helmets, combat boots, and carried M-14 or M-16 rifles, canteens, and hand grenades. Back in the world, young men and women wore love beads, psychedelic colored clothing, had long hair, and smoked pot.

Americans had been fighting in Southeast Asia since 1961. More than five hundred thousand men and women were deployed in Vietnam. And, some forty-five thousand Americans had died there. Tensions and antiwar sentiments had been building for some time and came to a boiling point on November 15, 1969, when more than two million people gathered in Washington, D.C., to protest the war in what was billed as the Vietnam Peace Moratorium.

More than two million people gathered in the nation's capital
to demonstrate against the Vietnam War, November 15, 1969.

It was the largest demonstration ever held in the United States. Attendees wore black armbands to signify their objection to the war. Buses were positioned bumper to bumper along "E" Street, 15th and 17th Streets, and Pennsylvania Avenue, bordering the White House, to keep the demonstrators at bay. Cpl Thompson, a member of the *Leatherneck* Magazine staff, and I were there with our cameras. We had the day off, but couldn't resist the opportunity to capture more Vietnam War history in photos.

The march to the Washington Monument took them past the White House,
adequately protected by buses parked bumper to bumper completely
surrounding the building and its property.

Demonstrations were conducted at the Capitol building and on the Mall near the Washington Monument and Lincoln Memorial. Cpl Thompson and I passed on the Capitol program. We photographed the march pass the White House and on to the Washington Monument. Along the way we were joined by an old friend from the war, Eddie Adams. The Pulitzer Prize winning photographer was covering the march and making photos for the AP.

Leatherneck Magazine staffer Sgt Paul Thompson (l)
and I ran into an old friend from Vietnam,
photographer Eddie Adams (r) while covering
the march on our spare time.

I picked up my orders to attend the 10th Warrant Officer Screening Course on December 5th. I had two days to report to the Marine Corps Development and Education Command at Quantico, Virginia.

From a rank standpoint, warrant officers are senior to all enlisted men and junior to second lieutenants. They have their own pay scale and enjoy a prestige all their own. Having been enlisted makes them sort of an unofficial link between the commander and his troops. It was a highly coveted position with only twelve hundred twenty-nine warrant officers on active duty in the Marine Corps in 1969.

The screening course at Quantico was six weeks long. It was

conducted at the Officer Candidate School. And, like boot camp, OCS was mentally and physically demanding. Additionally, a warrant officer candidate lost his enlisted rank and accompanying prestige while attending the screening course. Whether staff sergeant or gunny, it made no difference; at OCS you were nothing more than "Candidate" Jones.

Fourteen leadership traits were stressed at OCS, and while we were not tested on them in a written exam, we were observed each day, both by the platoon staff and by our fellow candidates. Our demonstrated traits played an important role in how far up the ladder we graduated.

Drill, functioning of the M-14 rifle, troop leading steps, and five paragraph order, map reading, compass, first aid, principles of leadership, cover and concealment, and physical conditioning were taught, learned, and demonstrated daily.

TBS rope climb.

What was the toughest part about OCS? If you asked a warrant officer what he remembered most about the screening course he probably said the "Hill Trail." We went on five forced marches and numerous "administrative moves" and saw so many hills it was easy to think Quantico was located in the heart of a mountain range instead of on the banks of the Potomac River in eastern Virginia.

The Hill Trail—the nemesis of both OCS
and The Basic School at Quantico.

With the exception of our final academic grade, the platoon commander "held the hammer." His evaluation of our leadership principles and physical prowess accounted for 50 percent of the final grade in each area. Our final standing in our platoon and company was determined by assigning a weight factor to each of the final grades. Leadership accounted for 50 percent of the final grade, with physical fitness accounting for 25 percent and academics the remaining 25 percent. The honor man of the company received an engraved wrist watch from the National Society, Daughters of the American Colonists.

The December 1969 issue of the *Leatherneck* Magazine hit the stands just before I arrived at Quantico. When Gen Walt, now a four star general and the Assistant Commandant of the Marine Corps, saw it, he sat down and penned a letter to me which I received a few days after beginning the screening course at Quantico.

> *Dear Sergeant Bowen,*
>
> *I have just finished reading your two articles ["Too Quiet, Too Long" and "Hope for Tomorrow"] in the Dec Leatherneck. I want to congratulate you on the excellence of these articles and on your reporting.*
>
> *Keep up the good work! More of this is what our country needs —*
>
> *Warm regards,*
>
> L. W. Walt

I received a footlocker full of good natured razzing when the platoon leader had me read the letter out loud to my platoon mates. Nonetheless, the letter was and is a prized possession. And, I'm sure the general's letter was taken into consideration when my back went out on the "Belly Robber" exercise contraption and I missed a few days of physical training.

Most of us completed the screening portion at Mainside with ease and moved on to the Warrant Officer Basic Class at Camp Barrett, also part of Quantico. There, we had an instructional staff that included officers that many of us had already met at some point in our careers.

All of the instructors had rows of ribbons attesting to their service in Vietnam, but most of the warrant officers had more decorations. Our group had at least one Navy Cross, several Silver Stars, and a host of Bronze Stars and Purple Hearts. One of our instructors, Captain Oliver North, appeared not to understand why we were not in awe over his awards and decorations, which included a Silver Star.

I was assigned as editor of our class booklet and given permission to carry a small camera to document our training during the ten-week course. I chose a Minox Spy Camera. It had a 15mm lens and used special film rated at ASA 125. It was the perfect size and weight (about six ounces) for a Marine otherwise weighed down with rifle, pack, steel helmet, canteen, and entrenching tool.

WOBC had a demanding curriculum. Night orienteering, crew-served weapons, forced marches, the rifle and pistol ranges, platoon and company combat tactics, and the construction of barbed wire barriers were part of our daily routine. One day, while on field maneuvers, I slipped on a flat rock while crossing a creek. I held my rifle high, avoiding any damage to the M-14, but landed on my left thigh. To this day, that thigh has a flat indention and very little feeling.

Observing 81mm mortar accuracy. The only man without binoculars was in the optical repair occupational field.

We graduated from the Screening Course at Little Hall on January 23, 1970. Major General Raymond Davis, Medal of Honor recipient for heroism in Korea, was the principle speaker. Gunny Tom Bartlett was on hand to throw me my first salute and accept my silver dollar. Then on to The Basic School for the Warrant Officer Basic Class 1-70. When we graduated from "knife and fork" school, as TBS was called, on April 9, Gunny Bartlett was again there to hand me my third set of orders to *Leatherneck* Magazine, this time as a special projects officer to oversee publication of a compilation of *Leatherneck* correspondent coverage of the Vietnam War we titled *Ambassadors in Green*.

The Basic School logo.

My enlisted service number, 1900274, was a thing of the past. From that point forward, I would be known as 0112892, my officer service number. That is until January 1972 when the Marine Corps did away with service numbers all together and began using social security numbers to identify its enlisted and officers.

Unbeknownst to me, CWO Bill Parker, Secretary-Treasurer of the Leatherneck Association, had sent a letter to HQMC, requesting that "upon graduation, WO Robert L. Bowen, be temporarily assigned to Leatherneck Magazine for a period of six months to produce a special edition commemorating six years of Marine Corps service in Vietnam."

CHAPTER 27

Leatherneck *Magazine—Special Assignment*

*Edit your manuscript until your fingers bleed and you have
memorized every last word. Then, when you are certain
you are on the verge of insanity . . . edit one more time.*
~ C. K. Webb, Author

Gunny Bartlett and I shared an office for my latest *Leatherneck* Magazine
assignment.

Gunny Tom Bartlett and WO Bob Bowen,
coauthors of *Ambassadors in Green.*

Ambassadors in Green was conceived of, written, designed, and produced by the two of us alone. And, it was our opportunity to put to use everything we had learned at Syracuse, New York. We tackled the task with gusto. We even finished it ahead of schedule despite repeated breaks for games of cribbage. After completing *Ambassadors in Green*, *Leatherneck* Magazine found another project for me.

Pictorial report of *Leatherneck* Magazine's
coverage of the Vietnam War.

In June, I was advanced in my former enlisted status to the rank of gunnery sergeant, E-7. It was a paper promotion only as I never actually wore the rank. But, having been selected for enlisted advancement at the same time I was chosen for the warrant officer screening program it was necessary to complete the enlisted process.

At some point in 1969, *Leatherneck* Magazine writers began holding Friday night poker games. Gunny Bartlett, Gunny Ed Evans, Sgt Martin, Sgt Thompson, Sgt Wolf, Sgt Giles, Sgt Gnatzig, and I were the principle players, but most games had only five or six players at one time. The game rotated amongst the players. The host would provide snacks and beer. The games were nickel-dime-quarter affairs and no one ever got rich or went to the poor house.

One night in 1970, after returning to the magazine as a warrant officer, Gunny Parker asked me if he could join a game. I was the host that night. Much to our surprise, when he arrived his wife, June, was with him. The wives seldom joined our games, but June wanted to play. How do you tell the boss's wife, "no"? She played.

As is customary with poker, the deal rotated and when it came time for June to deal, she deftly shuffled the deck, passed it to her left to be cut, then called her game and began to deal. "Seven-card stud," she announced with a smile, "whores, fours, and one-eyed jacks wild." You could have heard a pin drop until the men began coughing and knocking their stacked coins to the floor. We had a rule at our games. If any money fell on the floor it stayed on the floor. The children of the host would collect it in the morning. My kids swept up a bundle from the game the next morning.

The Leatherneck Association published the Marine's enlisted bible, *Guidebook for Marines.* It contained every subject a Marine needed to know, including first aid, hygiene and sanitation, drill, functioning of the rifle and pistol, and history and tradition, to name a few.

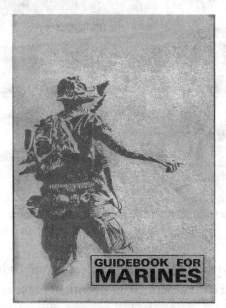

Basic military subjects every Marine needs
to survive in war and peace.

The *Guidebook* was updated periodically and 1970 was chosen for its latest editing. Only this time, it would receive a complete makeover. Instead of the customary left-right turning of the pages, the new *Guidebook* would be narrower and feature a vertical format with pages you flipped. This would make it easier for the Marine recruit undergoing boot camp to carry the book without folding it in his back pocket. It was also printed on a special waterproof paper.

In early 1971, I accompanied a young Marine writer, Sgt Gnatzig, on his first road assignment for the magazine. We went to California for stories on the boot camp at San Diego, the Communications-Electronics School at Twentynine Palms, the Horse Marines at Miramar Marine Corps Air Station, and the Marine Barracks at San Diego. I served as Sgt Gnatzig's photographer.

Miramar, California, near San Diego, home of
mounted horse Marines in the 1970s.

In addition to these articles, Sgt Gnatzig wrote a whimsical piece he titled "Dear Diary." It described an overnight horse ride we took with five mounted Marines into the hills surrounding the base. His report was whimsical. The ride was real.

Marines on patrol in the hills surrounding Miramar, 1971.
The area was a favorite hangout for the hippies of that era.

Sgt Gnatzig wrote in his diary:

We started out over a flat stretch of brushland at an "easy trot." It looked easy as these five Marines assumed rocking motions in their saddles. I was bouncing up and down with all the grace of a spastic grasshopper, in the air most of the time but meeting the saddle with great force on each downward movement.

I felt awfully conspicuous until I looked behind me to see Gunner Bowen having the same problem. If my optic nerve wasn't being shaken loose by my equestrian inability, he might even have looked funny.

But, after a couple miles we'd both gotten the knack of sitting on a trotting horse, our brains slowly unscrambled, and, we were, without a doubt, a couple of fine looking horsemen.

It was about this time that all five Marines went "Hiyagh!" and took their horses full tilt for the top of the nearest knoll.

I learned something about horses today. If you have seven trotting horses, and five start running at top speed, you don't have five running and two trotting. You have seven running as fast as their 28 legs will carry them.

In my free time back at the *Leatherneck* Magazine, I produced a special book of photos for Gen Walt. I presented it to him in his office on January 11, 1971. It contained copies of photos I had made of the general four years earlier in Vietnam and a few I made when I reported on his promotion to four-star general and assignment as Assistant Commandant of the Marine Corps two years earlier in 1969. In return, Gen Walt gave me an autographed copy of his book, *Strange War, Strange Strategy*. The "Four-Star Grunt," recipient of two Navy Cross medals for bravery in World War II and numerous other awards for service in Korea and Vietnam, retired in 1972. He had served thirty-six years as a Marine Corps officer. He died in 1989.

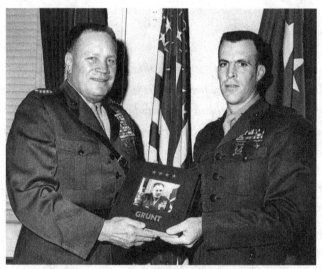

The author prepared a book of photos he had made of General Lewis W. Walt in Vietnam as a three-star and later as a four-star when he was promoted and elevated to the office of Assistant Commandant of the Marine Corps.

Recently promoted MSgt Bartlett and I also found time to take two trips to recognize friends who had worked, or still worked, for *Leatherneck* Magazine. SSgt Jim Elliott and Sgt Cherilee Noyes, both writers for the magazine, were married in early 1971. Sgt Noyes had gone to Vietnam to report on the women there, the only active duty woman Marine at the time to fully earn the title "Combat Correspondent." She and SSgt Elliott were married in Columbus, Ohio. Their reception was held at an American Legion post in an old Polish section of town. MSgt Bartlett and I drove to the wedding that morning. We left the reception early and traveled home that night.

In May of that year, we made another one-day trip, only this time it was to Syracuse, New York, where SSgt Bruce Martin was graduating from the Navy Program in Photojournalism. SSgt Martin was the fifth member of the *Leatherneck* Magazine staff to attend the special graduate-level, two-semester course.

MSgt Bartlett and I were awarded the Bronze Star with Combat V for our coverage of the war for *Leatherneck* Magazine from 1965 through 1969. We also received the Navy Achievement Medal for our work on *Ambassadors in Green.*

CHAPTER 28

Defense Information School

Information is the oxygen of the modern age.
It seeps through the walls topped by barbed wire,
it wafts across the electrified borders.
~ Ronald Reagan, 40th President of the United States

When my two special projects were completed at *Leatherneck* Magazine, I received orders to report to the Division of Information at Headquarters, Marine Corps, just across the street. Those orders were quickly followed by new instructions.

> You will proceed in time to report on 4 March 1971 to the Commandant, Defense Information School, Fort Benjamin Harrison, Indianapolis, Indiana, for temporary additional duty under instruction for a period of about eight weeks in the Information Officer Course.

The Marine Corps had decided it was time for me to go to school. I had been working as a Marine journalist without any MOS training for eleven years, but it was time for me to be schooled as a 4302, Information Officer.

Fort Benjamin Harrison was dubbed Uncle Ben's Rest Home. Land for the base was purchased in 1903 and the base was fully operational by 1908. It covered some three hundred sixty acres. During its illustrious service, the base served as home for Civilian Conservation Corps (CCC) workers, the Indiana National Guard, an airfield where the Tenth Air Force was headquartered, a Citizen's Civilian Military Camp, and a host of joint service military schools, including DINFOS, the Defense Information School.

Closed in 1991, the huge complex that was Fort Benjamin Harrison continues to play host to several military functions including the Army Finance Center, contained in the largest sole-purpose military building in the United States, including the Pentagon.

DINFOS had a varied curriculum. Courses were designed for officers and junior and senior enlisted. There were courses in print and broadcast journalism. The officers received a smidgen of both, but the emphasis for them was on running a public affairs office and interfacing with the community.

The eight-week officer course included instruction in the duties of a public affairs officer, policy and plans, writing, photography, community relations, and international relations and government. I was billeted in the transient officer quarters while attending DINFOS. The transient building bordered the grassy parade field. The building reeked of the smell of rice being cooked by allied officers from Thailand and Vietnam. They loved their rice and the exotic fish sauce called *nuoc mam*. The Thai fish sauce, equally caustic to the nose, was called *nam pla*.

The first morning there, when the base cannon was fired at 6:00 a.m. announcing reveille and the beginning of another day, I rolled out of bed and slid under my bunk. That was a normal reaction to that sound in Vietnam, and it was the first time I had heard a cannon fired since the last time I was in Vietnam in 1969. I resisted yelling "incoming!"

The allied officer in my class was West German Captain Christian von Stechow. He was an excellent representative for his country. He was articulate, accomplished in English, a good writer, and had good communication skills. He delighted us with his jokes, all of which we'd heard before, but when we told them it was always "how many Polish electricians does it take to change a light bulb" or some other similar question. When Capt von Stechow told the joke, "Polish" was replaced by "American."

I graduated with honors from the Defense Information School in the spring of 1971, and headed back to Headquarters Marine Corps for duty with the Division of Information (DivInfo).

When I left Indianapolis, the DINFOS Commandant, Air Force Colonel Frank Meek, told me not to make any firm housing commitments when I got back to HQMC. "I'm requesting that you return to relieve so and so, an Army O-5, as chief of the Photojournalism Division." A young Marine warrant officer relieve an Army lieutenant colonel? Never happen, I said to myself, but thanked the colonel for his faith in my abilities nonetheless.

I was at DivInfo for two months when I received orders to return to DINFOS for permanent assignment as Chief of the Photojournalism Division. The assignment included liaison duty with the annual DoD/ NPPA Flying Short Course in Photojournalism, the annual NPPA Newsfilm Workshop at Oklahoma University, Norman, and coordinator of the annual Military Photographer of the Year competition judged at the University of Missouri School of Journalism in Columbia.

The photojournalism instruction building had been a prison for German and Italian prisoners of war during World War II. The cells had been converted to individual instructor offices, supply rooms, and student photo darkrooms. Supply management and equipment accountability procedures were atrocious. And, during the most recent Inspector General's inspection, the photojournalism division had flunked, the only DINFOS office to suffer such an indignity. Remedying that situation became my first priority.

It was a fabulous assignment. I got to meet all of the young Marine writers on their way up, many noncommissioned officers coming back for senior courses, and young officers about to be assigned as PAOs for the first time. We did not teach only Marines. Our students came from every branch of the service and included DoD public affairs civilians. Allied officers also attended our courses.

I arrived in Indianapolis in August. The following month, I applied for the LDO (limited duty officer) program. My first Flying Short Course in Photojournalism was scheduled for October. The week-long traveling seminar began in Washington, D.C. Before leaving Indianapolis, I took my wife to the base hospital for a routine seventh-month, prenatal checkup. She was pregnant with what we thought was our fourth child.

DINFOS staff director Tom Harrell (l) and MGySgt Gus Apsitis
pin my collar bars on when I was promoted to LDO first lieutenant.
Harrell, a retired Marine major and combat correspondent in World War II,
was a member of the team that determined the curriculum
for DINFOS when it was established in 1965.

The following morning, while attending a briefing at the Pentagon, I received a call from DINFOS. My wife had just given birth to twin boys. "The hospital is calling them babies A and B until you guys name them," Captain Sara "Sally" Pritchett said. "And, because of their size they are being transferred to the Children's Hospital downtown. They are heathy. Just underweight."

Brian and Alan. It was easy to distinguish between these identical twins.
Alan had a birthmark beside his left eye.

After the seminar in Washington, D.C., the next day, we were scheduled to fly to Chicago for a day of instruction there. Chicago, Illinois, was less than two hundred miles north of Indianapolis. One of my instructors was willing to drive my car and meet me there. I could skip the Chicago course, return to Indianapolis for a quick visit to see my wife and two new sons, and return to Chicago the following day for the flight to Los Angeles, the final stop on our weeklong flying short course in photojournalism.

GySgt Lanny Slifer, senior enlisted Marine
photojournalism instructor at DINFOS.

The plan worked fine. Marine Gunnery Sergeant Lanny Slifer was there when my plane arrived in Chicago. We rushed to Indianapolis. The twins were officially named Alan and Brian. Alan weighed just over five pounds, but Brian was only four pounds, eleven ounces. The hospital refused to let them go home until both weighed more than five pounds. I returned to Chicago the next day and flew to the West Coast. By the time the trip was over, my wife and the twins had returned home. Our other three children had been taken in by members of the Photojournalism Division. Capt Pritchett had arranged for two months of free diaper service paid for by the entire DINFOS staff.

Captain Sara "Sally" Pritchett, Senior DINFOS Marine.

CHAPTER 29

Purple Suit Concept

You make different colors by combining
those colors that already exist.

~ Herbie Hancock, Pianist

The Defense Information School championed the purple suit concept. The idea was simple. If you took the colors of the military uniforms (Army, Navy, Air Force, Marine Corps, and Coast Guard) and mixed them all together, the color would be purple. Therefore, there should be only one kind of public affairs, writing and photography taught to and practiced by the various branches of the armed forces.

The photojournalism phase of the course for officers, enlisted, and civilians alike, focused on basic photographic skills, to include making the photo, processing the film, making contact sheets, printing, and producing a picture story, complete with words to describe whatever story the student had decided he or she wanted to tell.

Formal classroom instruction was conducted in a building a few hundred feet distant from the former World War II POW facility where the photo labs were located. It contained a huge working model of a Pentax 35mm camera—the same camera we issued to each of the students during the photojournalism phase of their instruction.

I welcomed each new class of students when they began their photojournalism instruction, but the curriculum was presented by the military and civilian instructors on the staff. My senior enlisted instructor was Navy Chief Frank Powers. He was assisted by Marine Gunny Slifer, Marine Staff Sergeant Bob Wilson, Navy Petty Officer First Class Lonnie McKay, Navy Petty Officer Second Class Duncan Campbell, and civilians Dale Schofner and Floyd Shively. Air Force Master Sergeant Skip Greene taught a special motion picture class for the officers.

The bulk of my work at DINFOS was serving as Department of Defense liaison with civilian groups assisting DoD with its educational pursuits in the field of visual communications, be it still or motion. Each year, I devoted a good portion of my time to three endeavors: the Flying Short Course in Photojournalism, the TV Newsfilm Workshop, and the Military Pictures of the Year Competition.

The Flying Short Course in Photojournalism was described briefly in the previous chapter. Each year, normally in the fall, the NPPA chose three or four cities for a one-day seminar. The instructors came from throughout the visual communication industry. Newspaper, magazines, television stations, camera makers, and photo supply manufacturers were included.

Flying Short Courses were not conducted in 1972, but we made up for it by conducting two weeklong flying courses in 1973, one in the United States and one in Europe. The stateside courses were always open to both military and civilian photographers and writers. The European venture was strictly for the military.

The European tour took place in April. It included stops at Lakenheath Air Base, England; Frankfort, Germany; Ramstein Air Base, Germany; and Naples, Italy. The instructor staff included yours truly; Professor Dick Yoakam, Indiana University, Bloomington; Jack Bradley, photographer for the Peoria, Illinois *Journal Star*; Michael Kalush of WXYZ Television in Detroit, Michigan; John Fletcher of the *National Geographic* Magazine; and Barry Edmonds, photographer of the Flint, Michigan *Journal*. Army Major James Durham of the Assistant Secretary of Defense for Public Affairs was the project officer.

Instructor staff for the special 1973 European Military Flying Short Course in Photojournalism (l-r): Barry Edmonds, John Fletcher, the author, Jack Bradley, Mike Kalush, Maj Jim Durham, and Professor Dick Yoakum.

When not teaching, we did what most Americans do in Europe. We went sightseeing. In England, we took a taxi from Lakenheath, down the famous "crooked mile" road to a 14th century roadhouse that had been converted into a restaurant. There, I was introduced to escargot and could not get enough of the tasty snails. They became my meal of choice at every stop.

We visited a bruhaus in Frankfort to hear some traditional German music and since we were unfamiliar with German money we wound up paying an arm and a leg for some pretzels. In fact, we bought the entire platter.

We traveled from Frankfort to Ramstein in one of the trains Hitler had used during World War II. He had named the train "America." We flew from Ramstein to Naples and our air route took us over the Alps of Switzerland.

When not teaching in Naples, we spent most of our time walking around the seaport town making photos. One afternoon, we traveled to Rome for a riding tour of Italy's largest city and its capitol.

Our Flying Short Course in Photojournalism seminars were conducted in four cities that year—Newark, New Jersey; Indianapolis, Indiana; Houston, Texas; and Seattle, Washington.

In 1972, 1973, and 1974, Gunny Slifer and I drove to Norman,

Oklahoma, for a weekend Television Newsfilm Workshop conducted at the University of Oklahoma Center for Continuing Education by the NPPA. We served as members of the film critique staff and provided the film editing stations used by the students to prepare their film for presentation and judging.

The instructors also received certificates for the TV Newsfilm Workshop.

Each year, the DoD joined with the NPPA, Kodak, Nikon Camera, and the University of Missouri School of Journalism to select a "Military Photographer of the Year." Entries were sent initially to DINFOS where they were logged in for further transportation to the school in Columbia, Missouri, for judging. That was one of my "other duties as assigned." I found the experience especially rewarding since I had been chosen as a runner up to the Military Photographer of the Year award in 1967.

Professor Cliff Edom, the head of the photojournalism department at the University of Missouri, School of Journalism, was known as the "Father of Photojournalism" having coined the term in the 1950s. He was highly respected through the field. Professor Edom was still in charge of the photojournalism program at Missouri in the 1970s and he coordinated getting the judges together one day in April each year.

Judging the Military Photographer of the Year competition at the
University of Missouri School of Journalism in 1972.
Professor Cliff Edom, Father of Photojournalism, is at the right.

In 1972, Professor Edom surprised me when he asked me to accompany him and his wife, Vi, to one of the school darkrooms. There, he submerged my right hand in a tray of hypo, mumbled a few words, and declared me a member of Kappa Alpha Mu, the Honorary Fraternity of Photojournalism. Other members included Margret Burke White, Ansel Adams, Carl Steichen, David Douglas Duncan, and a host of other famous photographers.

To reward my secretary for good work throughout the year, I took her to the judging in 1973. Doris Litherland helped organize the entries by category and assisted in presenting them to the judges for their viewing.

In the fall of 1973, I was recruited by Vincennes University, Vincennes, Indiana, to teach a special course in basic photography for civilians and members of the military assigned to Fort Benjamin Harrison. My teaching the eight-week course was approved by the DINFOS leadership and the classes were conducted at night. The University paid me for my effort.

Kappa Alpha Mu key fob.

In January 1974, I was the guest speaker for the Indiana Business Communicators. I titled my talk "The Care and Feeding of Photos."

My old 6th grade classmate, SSgt Bice showed up at DINFOS in the spring of 1974. He had put his infantryman MOS, 0369, on the shelf and was transitioning into the public affairs field, 4300. It was as if every time I moved, SSgt Bice was just around the corner. As I recall, he made it through the basic course with ease. Must have been his early schooling from Mrs. Harris, our 6th grade teacher.

Donkey basketball visited Fort Benjamin Harrison in June 1974, shortly before I was scheduled to leave for my next duty as station manager of the Far East Network at Misawa Air Base, Japan. DINFOS entered a team. Yours truly was a member.

My donkey did not like me. At least that's my excuse. Midway through the first period, the animal bucked, tossing me to the floor. I landed on my right elbow and chipped the bone. I grinned, in pain, but sought no medical attention. I didn't want anything to interfere with the travel plans already arranged to whisk me to Japan in two days.

Don't remember who won the game or if a winner was declared, but
this donkey threw the author who wound up with a chipped elbow.
The kids enjoyed the brouhaha.

When I left DINFOS I was awarded my second Navy Achievement
Medal.

CHAPTER 30

Far East Network: Misawa Air Base, Japan

Television news is like a lightning flash.
It makes a loud noise, lights up everything around it, leaves
everything else in darkness, and then is suddenly gone.
~ Hodding Carter

I was at DINFOS from August 1971 until June 1974, when my family boarded a plane bound for Misawa Air Base, Japan. I was sent to relieve Chief Warrant Officer Larry LePage as station manager of the Far East Network Radio and Television Station. CWO LePage was Capt Arnold's assistant ISO in Vietnam, so relieving CWO LePage in Misawa served as a reunion of sorts. Ironically, Capt Arnold had also served as the station manager of FEN, Misawa just prior to going to Vietnam.

The first order of business after arriving in Japan was to visit the hospital to check on my elbow. It had begun locking up since my tumble during a game of "donkey basketball" before leaving the States. The floating chip occasionally got inside the elbow joint making it impossible to move the arm without severe pain. A quick outpatient visit to the Misawa Air Base hospital took care of the problem. The doctor made a small incision, removed the chip, and I went to work, pain free.

Getting acquainted with my new office, July 1974.

Misawa was one of those "best kept secret" assignments. In the 1970s, the base contained elements of all four services, plus the Japanese Air Self Defense Force. With the exception of those of us at FEN, the men and women at Misawa were engaged primarily in security missions. Most of the Air Force personnel belonged to USAFSS, the United States Air Force Security Service. Sailors were assigned to USNSGA, or the Naval Air Station. The Navy flew Lockheed P-3 Orion antisubmarine and maritime surveillance aircraft throughout the area.

The Army had its Military Intelligence Detachment and the Marines had Company E, Marine Security Battalion, all involved in keeping watch on North Korea, China, and the Soviet Union. Counting dependents, the base was "home away from home" for less than five thousand Americans.

My staff at Misawa included members of all four services, most of whom I still communicate with today. We survived several earthquakes that sent our film racks and television cameras crashing to the studio floor. We also had to contend with snows that began in October and didn't fully melt until the following May.

July 1974–May 1977 was an interesting time in our history and being the primary source of news for Americans stationed at Misawa was both challenging and rewarding.

President Nixon resigned and was pardoned by President Gerald Ford in 1974. Hank Aaron surpassed Babe Ruth's home run record that year. Spain's General Francisco Franco died in 1975. Saigon fell to the North Vietnamese that year and combat Marines were the focus of what became known as the Mayaguez Incident after Khmer Rouge rebels took control of Cambodia.

FEN Marines joined with Company E Marines to celebrate the Corps' 200th birthday on November 10, 1975. I served as Adjutant for the Marine Corps Ball, reading the Commandant's message. My 6th-grade buddy, SSgt Sonny Bice, won the heavyweight boxing championship of the Marine Corps that year. He was four months shy of his 36th birthday.

Nearly 23,000 people were killed in an earthquake in Guatemala and Honduras in February 1976. FEN organized a telethon to help raise money for the survivors. Apple Computer launched in April 1976, creating an earthquake of its own within the computer industry.

Reading the Commandant's message at the 200th birthday celebration of the Marine Corps, November 10, 1776.

Jimmy Carter was inaugurated as the 39th President of the United States in January 1977. Almost immediately he pardoned all Vietnam War draft dodgers who had not been involved in violent acts, a decision that raised the hackles of most active duty men and women, and military veterans. And, Alex Haley was awarded a special Pulitzer Prize for his book, *Roots*.

FEN covered it all. We were the primary source for all English-language news, music, sports, and old and new American television programs. Marines at FEN at the time included Staff Sergeant Herman Lange and Sergeants John Wilson, Joe Sigillo, and Dick Bugda. (Both Lange and Bugda retired as sergeants major. Wilson and Sigillo did not retire but were promoted to staff sergeant before they left the Corps.)

Discussing production in radio studio with Sgt John Wilson.

Air Force Colonel Lester Mellott was commander of the 6921st Security Wing for most of the time I was there. He hosted a monthly breakfast at the officer club for his tenant commanders. This gave us an opportunity to air any concerns we might have, on any subject, in an unofficial way.

One morning in early 1975, we arrived and discovered that Col Mellott had invited Korean Reverend Myung Moon to our breakfast. Reverend Moon was head of the Unification Church and specialized in conducting mass weddings. I don't recall any grievances being aired that day.

I was promoted to captain while at Misawa, an interesting rank for someone who had frequent dealings with the Yokosuka Navy Base near Tokyo. The personnel records of the sailors assigned to FEN were maintained there. In the Navy, a captain is an O-6, the equivalent of a colonel. When I placed a call to the Navy at Yokosuka, I simply identified myself as Captain Bowen. Invariably the Yeoman who answered the call visualized a four-stripper and my request received a prompt and satisfactory response.

My son's fifth grade class went to Sapporo in 1976 to see the Snow Festival held there in February each year. I went along as a chaperon. The festival showcased the work of Japanese artists who fashioned massive ice sculptures of Japanese Gods, cartoon characters, and to help honor America's Bicentennial year, famous buildings in Washington, D.C.—the Capitol, the White House, and the Lincoln Memorial.

Chaperone for son, Jack's fifth grade class trip to Sapporo Snow Festival in 1976 (l-r): Vic Moreno, Bryan Lopez, Jack, the brave one.

It was my second trip to the northern Japanese island of Hokkaido. Shortly after arriving in 1974, I traveled to the small Japanese town of Chitose. The United States had operated a small air base there, complete with a FEN radio station, but it had been closed. So, one of my Japanese engineers accompanied me there to remove the usable equipment left behind.

I was introduced to sushi on that trip, but the featured item on the menu at the small sushi house we stopped at was fish eyes. I managed to get one pair down, but never again. I didn't like the idea of what I was eating staring back at me.

We had arrived in July. The following month, my wife's mother passed away on Okinawa. The kids went to Sgt Wilson's home while my wife and I caught "hops" to Okinawa for the wake and cremation. We returned inside of a week.

At first we lived right across the street from the Officers Club. Cats were plentiful on base, especially the Siamese breed, and one of them adopted us. We named her Yuki and as females are inclined to do, she promptly became pregnant. Since we lived so close to the "O" Club we didn't get a baby sitter when we went cross the street to celebrate the arrival of 1975.

CTR2, Cryptologic Technician (Collection), Tim Smith, on bass guitar,
and The Sundowners were regular performers at FEN,
especially during telethons such as those conducted
for Guatemala relief and Operation Eyesight.

Around 10 p.m., the club phone operator announced that there was a call for Capt Bowen. Number one son, Jack, was on the line to announce the arrival of Yuki's first kitten. The call was repeated three or four more times, and by then everyone at the New Year's Eve Ball knew what was happening. When the final call came through, there was no call to pick up the phone. The operator simply announced so all could hear, "Capt Bowen, you have another kitten."

Sgt Wilson and his wife, Jan, liked the maturity of our only daughter, Donna, and when she turned ten in 1976, they began calling on her to babysit their daughter, Lynn. Jan recently offered the following assessment of why she would trust her newborn to a ten-year-old: "Responsible, loving, makes sure everyone is safe, always watching everything, big sisterly, and mature beyond her years. I knew that when we left, she was in control! Compare that to today's kids it wouldn't happen."

Each year, company grade officers at Misawa (lieutenants and captains) organized a Misawa Snow Festival. It was fashioned after Japan's Sapporo Snow Festival, but on a much smaller scale. I was in charge of the festival in 1976. We enlisted the help of the flight line snow removal crew to gather the snow we needed to build our displays. Each unit on base joined in to produce a display of their choosing.

Mustangs, officers who served previously as enlisted, never forget their roots. And, while they do not traditionally associate with enlisted men or women, Misawa was a small base, and there were only a handful of Marine officers stationed there. So, my main friends there were two senior Air Force broadcasters, Technical Sergeants Bill Doolittle and Walter Smith, and Marine Sgt John Wilson.

TSgt Walt Smith prepares script for his "Swap Shop" show.

TSgt Doolittle and I were the closest. He and I watched sumo tournaments on Japanese television at the VFW post in town. We even traveled to Tokyo once to see a tournament.

TSgt Bill Doolittle cues up a record for his afternoon show.

I took up golf while at Misawa, and while not good at it, enjoyed the exercise and keeping track of where my ball went. I had played my first game of golf ten years earlier on Bermuda, slicing, hooking, and losing an entire package of twelve golf balls by the time I reached the 9th hole.

I learned to control my swing at Misawa's Gosser Memorial Golf Course. Built in 1956, the 18-hole course was five thousand, nine hundred eighty-three yards long. The fairways were lined with tall pine trees which were occupied by hundreds of Ravens. The birds liked watching the game being played and much like Heckle and Jeckle appeared to laugh with glee when a golfer screwed up.

One day, after teeing off on the second hole, a Raven flew to my ball, picked it up in its beak and began flying all over the course with me in hot pursuit in my golf cart. The large black bird would fly a few hundred feet, cover the ball with pine needles. When I approached it would snatch the ball up and fly off another distance. Eventually, the Raven flew to the top of a large pine and dropped the ball in its nest, leaving me with the age old problem of where to put my lost ball so I could continue to play the hole.

In November 1976, I became a Freemason and a member of Aomori Lodge #10. I was elected chaplain and installed in January, 1977.

Raised a Freemason 1976. Top row (l): Elected Chaplain
of Aomori Lodge #10, January 1977

I left Japan in May of that year, bound for the Pentagon and duty as the Marine Corps spokesman for the Secretary of Defense. My work at Misawa had been rewarded with the FEN Commanders Trophy and the Air Force Meritorious Service Medal.

⤐ CHAPTER 31 ⤏

Pentagon

*By early 1943, the Pentagon was complete—a building
big enough to house forty thousand people and all
their accoutrements, the largest building in the world
conceived, designed, and constructed in a little more
than a year. And the day it was completed,
it was already too small.*

~ David Brinkley, Newsman

I arrived at the Pentagon and assumed my duties as the Marine Desk
Officer in June 1977. As a captain, I was the junior officer in the
Defense Directorate of Information (DDI). The Army and Air Force
desks were manned by lieutenant colonels. The Navy desk officer was
a commander. The officer-in-charge of DDI was a full colonel.

Pentagon.

The Marine Desk responded to all media questions dealing with the Marine Corps, all joint service training exercises, those involving foreign troops, questions about military helping in humanitarian operations, and from time to time, "duties as assigned."

I had joined the Marine Corps Combat Correspondents Association when assigned to *Leatherneck* Magazine ten years earlier. When I arrived at the Pentagon, the local Jim Lucas Chapter of the USMCCCA was preparing to host the 1977 annual conference.

The National President, retired Master Gunnery Sergeant Jim Keyser, called and asked if I would take charge of judging photo entries in the contests the Combat Correspondent conducted each year. I agreed as long as he would assist. He agreed and the judging took place at my American Legion post in Woodbridge, Virginia, one Saturday morning.

The Jim Lucas Chapter President, CWO Bob Neely, then contacted me. He was preparing to assume the national presidency of the Combat Correspondents and was looking for a replacement as chapter president. Having served in that role at DINFOS in 1971, CWO Neely said I was the man to replace him. I let him twist my arm and when the Marine CCs gathered in Arlington in August 1977, I was there as president of the host chapter to greet them.

My old buddy, Marine CWO Dale Dye attended that year and entertained the assembled Marines at the annual banquet. His recitation of "Captain Jimmy Bones and his Devil Dog Marines" had his captive audience in awe. CWO Dye didn't miss a single line of the two thousand six hundred seven-word ballad.

Colonel Margaret A. Brewer was serving as Director of Women Marines when I arrived at the Pentagon, but on May 11, 1978, she was promoted to brigadier general, the first woman Marine to attain that rank, and appointed Director of Information.

CWO Dale Dye entertained the assembled Maine Corps Combat
Correspondents at their annual gathering in Arlington, 1977.

BGen Margaret Brewer, first Woman Marine promoted
to the general officer ranks.

Following my judging stint for the Marine Corps Combat
Correspondents the previous year, I was called on to judge Marine
Corps broadcast entries in the 1978 Thomas Jefferson Awards Program.
BGen Brewer thanked me for my assistance and said,

As an active duty Marine in the Public Affairs field, you continuously show a high degree of professionalism, as you did while judging the Marine Corps' entries for the all-service competition.

Everyone in DDI stood duty at the Pentagon when his or her name came up. This involved being the DoD spokesman for all media queries that arrived after normal working hours during week days and on the weekends. We were an 8–5 office, but in reality we were available 24–7. The duty officer would remain at his desk until 6:00 p.m., then go home and remain there—on call—for any media questions directed to the Pentagon until his tour of duty ended.

I was at home on duty the weekend of November 17–19, 1978. On Saturday, November 18, in Jonestown, Guyana, the Reverend Jimmy Jones ordered that visiting California Congressman Leo Ryan be killed. Reverend Jones was an American cult leader. He was the founder and leader of the Peoples Temple, based in San Francisco, California.

The Reverend Jim Jones ordered his followers to kill visiting Congressman Leo Ryan and then to commit suicide in Jonestown, Guyana. More than 900 died.

Reverend Jones had ordered the construction of Jonestown in Guyana two months earlier. Soon, rumors began running rampant that Jones was physically, mentally, and sexually abusing his followers. In November, Congressman Ryan led a fact-finding mission to

Jonestown to investigate allegations of human rights abuses. The delegation included relatives of Temple members. The group arrived in Georgetown, the capital of Guyana, on November 15. Two days later, they flew to Port Kaituma, a short distance from Jonestown.

Reverend Jones hosted a reception for the delegation that night. Congressman Ryan hastily left the compound that afternoon after being attacked with a knife yielded by a Temple member. Some fifteen Temple members had decided to leave with Congressman Ryan. Initially, Reverend Jones did not interfere with his followers' plans. But, after arriving back at the airfield at Port Kaituma, Jones' armed guard arrived and began shooting at the delegation. Congressman Ryan and four others were killed.

Back at the compound, Reverend Jones ordered his nine hundred eighteen followers to commit suicide by drinking grape-flavored Kool-Aid laced with cyanide. Nine hundred and nine complied with the order, including three hundred and four children. It was the greatest single loss of American civilian life in a deliberate act until 9/11, twenty-three years later.

An officer in the National Military Command Center called me at home. He informed me of what had occurred and suggested I get to my office at the Pentagon ASAP. "The phones are ringing off the hook," he said.

I called my immediate boss, Army Lieutenant Colonel Don Wakefield. He said to call him back when I arrived and he'd have a list of Qs & As (questions and answers) for me to use when the media called. The Army dispatched a team of soldiers from Fort Bragg, North Carolina. The soldiers placed the victims in body bags and prepared them for transport to the United States for processing at the Dover Air Force Base Mortuary, Dover, Delaware.

By Monday, November 20, the recovery operation was in full swing. The Army and Air Force desk officers at DDI assumed their responsibilities and were responding to service-specific questions. I could breathe easier for a while. However, I was back on duty Thanksgiving Day as the operation wound down.

The following month I received a memorandum from Tom

Lambert, Principle Deputy Assistant Secretary of Defense for Public Affairs:

> *I extend to you my appreciation for your outstanding efforts while serving as duty officer on two occasions during the Guyana Humanitarian Assistance Operation. At the outset and on Thanksgiving Day your assistance was of inestimable value to me.*

It's nice to have your work appreciated.

CHAPTER 32

Bobby Garwood Surfaces

Was Bobby Garwood a collaborator?
I believe the answer is "No."
He was a survivor caught up in a political game.
~ James Webb, Former Secretary of the Navy and U.S. Senator

In January 1979, Marine Private First Class Bobby Garwood passed a note to Finnish diplomat Ossi Rahkonen in Hanoi. PFC Garwood had been held as a prisoner of war in Vietnam when five hundred ninety-one American POWs were released between February and April 1973. PFC Garwood was captured in 1965 when he was nineteen-years old. He had been held for fourteen years. He was now thirty-three years old. He wanted to come home.

The American intelligence community knew of PFC Garwood's existence, but had not made it an issue. The long, bitter Vietnam War was over. Best to keep it that way. With PFC Garwood's public surfacing at a hotel in Hanoi on February 1, 1979, the cat was out of the bag. Hanoi confirmed Garwood's existence on February 26, but refused to identify him as a POW. DoD's dilemma now was how to explain him.

At the time of the 1973 prisoner release President Nixon and Secretary of State Henry Kissinger declared there were no more American POWs in Vietnam. Now, six years later, PFC Garwood had surfaced. If he wasn't a POW, what was he? Alabama Congressman

Sonny Montgomery said PFC Garwood was a deserter and if he came home he should be put in jail.

DoD and the Marine Corps quickly assembled a team to go to Bangkok to receive PFC Garwood when he arrived from Hanoi. Captain Joe Composto, a Marine JAG officer, was assigned as his counsel. Gunnery Sergeant David Langlois was assigned as his escort. I was assigned to represent the Assistant Secretary of Defense for Public Affairs and respond to all on-scene media queries.

We flew first to Okinawa for briefings at Third Marine Division headquarters. A representative from the 3rd MarDiv joined the recovery team and we flew on to Bangkok to pick up PFC Garwood. It was March 15. We waited on the military side of Bangkok's Don Muang International Airport for PFC Garwood's Air France flight from Hanoi. He didn't arrive. The American Consul General in Bangkok, Andrew Antippas, drove to our plane to let us know that the North Vietnamese refused to release PFC Garwood as long as the media continued to call him an American POW. It was too late to fly back to Okinawa, so we spent the night at the Imperial Hotel and flew back to Okinawa the following day.

I spent the next five days briefing newsmen on Okinawa and my bosses back in Washington, D.C. Since PFC Garwood was a Marine, and with me away from the Pentagon, the Marine Corps was handling all press queries back home. Lieutenant Colonel Arthur P. Brill, the spokesman at Headquarters Marine Corps, had this responsibility and I briefed him each morning and late afternoon, his time. Okinawa is thirteen hours ahead of Eastern Standard Time. The Officer in Charge of the Armed Forces Radio and Television Station, Marine Capt Dale Dye, an old friend, let me use his office for those overseas phone calls.

News reports about the "American POW" eased off, the North Vietnamese relented and on March 22, we flew back to Bangkok to get PFC Garwood. Gunny Langlois met him at the door, escorted by Counsel Antipas. After PFC Garwood was on the C-130, Gunny Langlois read him his rights and told him he was suspected of desertion. I signed the Article 31 document (military equivalent to a Miranda warning) as a witness to PFC Garwood's signature indicating he understood his rights against self-incrimination. Capt Composto cautioned him about saying anything that might be used against him.

Gunny David Langlois meets PFC Bobby Garwood and State Department envoy Andy Antipas when they arrive at the Marine C-130 for further transportation to Okinawa.

PFC Bobby Garwood signs the Article 31 document indicating that he understands the process he's undergoing while his attorney Capt Joe Composto, and Gunny David Langlois look on.

241

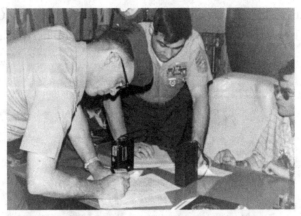

PFC Bobby Garwood (r) looks on as I witness
the signatures on the Article 31.

Gunny Langlois then gave PFC Garwood a photo album his family
had prepared for the day of his release. His mom had died while he was
in captivity. He was also given a few letters written to him by members of
his family. Through teary eyes, PFC Garwood brought himself up to date
with his Adams, Indiana, family. Adams was a small farming community
about five miles west-northwest of Greensburg where Bobby was born.
"Very strict Baptist community," Bobby would later recall.

The official paperwork transfer from North Vietnam to the U.S.
State Department to the Marine Corps took about two hours. PFC
Garwood boarded the C-130 at 4:00 p.m. We pulled up flaps and
departed Bangkok at 5:40 p.m.

PFC Garwood had very little with him when he boarded the plane.
He had a bottle of wine given him by the Air France plane captain, an
orchid given him by one of the Air France stewardesses, and a brown
vinyl jacket. He had nothing to eat so when the rest of us opened the
box lunches we had brought with us, we all found something to share
with him. Gunny Langlois had an extra peanut butter sandwich. Capt
Composto gave him a couple of Oreo cookies. I gave him a can of
Beanee Weenees. This was Bobby's first American meal in fourteen
years! Bobby "repaid" the kindness with some North Vietnam script
money he had in his pocket. He gave me an unopened pack of North
Vietnamese cigarettes.

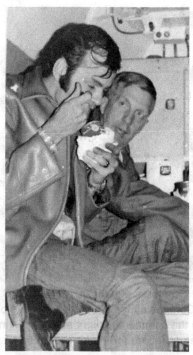

PFC Garwood enjoys his fist American meal after
14 years in captivity—a can of Beanee Weenees.

When we arrived on Okinawa, PFC Garwood was taken to the Army hospital at Camp Kuwae where he was given a complete physical and fitted for a new uniform. This took two days.

I spoke to the news media after arriving on Okinawa. The AP reported on March 23, "Charges were brought on the basis of allegations by other returning prisoners of war," said the spokesman, Capt. Bob Bowen. "There will be formal investigations to see whether we can go ahead with court-martial proceedings."

We left Naha, Okinawa, on a Northwest Airlines flight on March 24. We had a brief layover in Tokyo, but learning that the media was at the terminal hoping to interview PFC Garwood and get some photos, I arranged for us to remain on the plane. The next time we breathed fresh air was when we landed in Chicago the following day.

Shave, haircut, new uniform, and all smiles from PFC Bobby Garwood,
Capt Joe Composto, and Gunny David Langlois as they
board the commercial flight at Naha, Okinawa,
and prepare for the long flight home.

LtCol Brill was there working with the media. PFC Garwood told the waiting reporters "I love America." Then he was taken to the hospital's twelfth floor where he was reunited with his family.

The AP reported on PFC Garwood's arrival in Chicago. "Marine officials said PFC Garwood read letters from his family during the plane trip (from Bangkok to Okinawa). 'They brought tears to his eyes, knowing that his family still supported him,' said Marine Captain Bob Bowen who accompanied PFC Garwood."

I got on the next available flight and returned home to Washington, D.C. I had been on the road for better than two weeks.

PFC Garwood was eventually charged with desertion, but two years later the charges were dropped for lack of evidence. On February 5, 1981, he was found guilty of collaborating with the enemy. His lawyer appealed and that appeal is still pending more than thirty years later. PFC Garwood did not receive any back pay for his fourteen years in captivity.

Over the past few years I have become reacquainted with Bobby Garwood. We exchange emails and phone calls frequently—two old

Marines reliving a slice of their life from more than thirty-five years ago. In 2012, he joined my wife and me for lunch at a Cracker Barrel restaurant as we drove through southern Mississippi.

After a Cracker Barrel reunion with
Bobby Garwood in Mississippi, 2012.

I had no sooner returned from helping escort PFC Garwood than I was assigned as DoD spokesman for military involvement in the Skylab Reentry Project. NASA launched Skylab, an orbiting space laboratory, in May 1973. It was designed to remain in orbit until 1983, giving astronauts the opportunity to conduct scientific experiments.

Skylab, NASA's first orbiting space station.

Skylab was America's first space station. While in orbit, three separate three-man teams of scientist-astronauts were deployed onboard the spacecraft. Among other discoveries, a telescope system permitted the astronauts to confirm the existence of coronal holes in the Sun.

In December the previous year, NASA announced that due to uncertainties which had developed in the Skylab system, planning for further missions had been terminated and Skylab would be permitted to drop out of earth orbit. Elaborate plans were developed to track reentry into earth's atmosphere.

Naval ships were deployed throughout the anticipated Skylab crash site, but efforts to influence reentry were impossible. NASA had hoped to guide the spacecraft to a spot eight hundred ten miles south-southeast of Cape Town, South Africa.

Reentry began on July 11, 1979. Dozens of colorful firework-like flares were seen when the space station broke up in the atmosphere. Skylab debris landed southeast of Perth in western Australia. The debris path was from between Esperance to Rawlinna, a distance of some two hundred fifty miles as the crow flies. Twenty-four pieces of Skylab were found on one property in Esperance.

Analysis of some debris indicated that the space station had disintegrated ten miles above the Earth, much lower than expected. Skylab weighed one hundred seventy thousand pounds. It had been in orbit two thousand, two hundred forty-nine days and had been occupied by astronauts for one hundred seventy-one cumulative days. No one was injured during reentry.

I had joined the American Legion in 1974 while stationed at Misawa Air Base, Japan. I was a charter member of Vietnam Veterans Post 47 located there. When I returned home in 1977, I transferred my membership to Post 364 in Woodbridge, Virginia. In June 1980, I was installed as the Post's first active duty Vietnam veteran commander. Several coworkers from the Pentagon attended my installation.

Virginia State Vice Commander, Harry P. Graul, installed me as
Commander of American Legion Post 364, July 1979.

Pentagon desk officers answered every type of news media query
and made every kind of news announcement. In 1979 and 1980, we
were inundated with a series of Harrier crashes that had Congress and
many citizens wondering if the new vertical takeoff plane was what the
Marine Corps really needed. As the Pentagon's Marine spokesman, I
was the point person for responding to the Harrier concerns.

Early one morning in mid-April 1980, I had the opportunity to
respond to a Navy helicopter accident. The AP reported at 11:15 a.m.
April 16 that:

> *A Navy utility helicopter caught fire over commuter-crowded
> highways today, but landed on the Pentagon helipad where firemen
> extinguished the blaze without injury to the four crewmen.*
>
> *Capt. Robert Bowen, a Pentagon spokesman, said "the Navy H-3
> helicopter caught fire while on its' way to refuel after discharging
> Navy passengers near the Pentagon. The extent of the damage has
> not yet been determined.*

The Pentagon's helipad is located on the west side of the huge five-sided military office building. Twenty-one years later that same area would be the target of an airborne terrorist attack that claimed the lives of one hundred eighty-nine people—one hundred twenty-five of them members of the military stationed at the Pentagon, fifty-three passengers, six crew members on the plane, and five Al-Qaeda terrorists.

In January 1980, I submitted my letter of intent to retire later that year. I would have twenty years of military service at the end of July. The major promotion board was to meet that year and I was the senior captain in my occupational field. Promotion to major was a "shoo in," but I was thirty-nine-years old and I reasoned I would have a better chance of finding a civilian job at thirty-nine than I would at forty or older.

After submitting my letter, I prepared an SF-171, a standard government form used to list your qualifications for employment as a government employee. My goal was to be employed as a government writer or public affairs officer after I retired from the Marine Corps. Soon after I submitted the paperwork to the Office of Personnel Management, President Carter froze all government hiring.

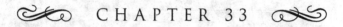

CHAPTER 33

Hostages and Refugees

Hostage is a mutant creation filled with fear,
self-loathing, guilt and death-wishing.
But he is a man, a rare, unique and beautiful
creation of which these things are no part.
~ Brian Keenan, Irish Writer

Two highlights remain for my tour at the Pentagon, my final Marine Corps assignment. I was at home, the on-call duty officer, on April 24, 1980. The National Military Command Center (NMCC) called to inform me there had been an accident during an attempt to rescue fifty-two American hostages in Iran. The caller gave no further details, but said to get to the Pentagon as soon as possible.

I called Air Force Lieutenant Colonel Michael I. Burch, who lived nearby. LtCol Burch worked in the operations office in DDI, the office that handles the classified side of our public affairs job. He told me to pick him up on the way to the Pentagon, which I did. I'm glad there were no state troopers on I-95 that night. We drove the thirty-five miles in record time.

This was the abortive Operation Eagle Claw. It involved a troop transport plane and eight helicopters. Three of the choppers were deemed unfit for the mission when it came time to launch. The remaining five were insufficient to continue from the desert to Tehran, so President Carter told them to stand down.

The rescue effort for American hostages in Tehran known
as Operation Eagle Claw ended in disaster on the desert,
April 28, 1980. Eight Delta Force soldiers were killed.

When they attempted to withdraw, one of the choppers clipped the
transport plane that had landed at the desert rendezvous point, catching
it on fire. The plane was loaded with Delta Force troops and aviation
fuel. Eight soldiers were killed. Both aircraft were destroyed.

LtCol Burch handled most of the media queries that night. I had a
top secret clearance, but this was an extremely sensitive operation and
I did not have the "need to know" for much of this one. (An example
of the Marine Corps Combat Correspondent motto of "First to Go,
Last to Know.")

April 1980 was a very busy month. The Cuban economy was at
rock bottom. About ten thousand Cubans had sought asylum in the
Peruvian embassy in Havana. On April 15, the Cuban government
launched the Mariel boatlift. Cuban President Fidel Castro said
any Cuban who wanted to leave the island could go to the Port of
Mariel, get on a boat, and sail to Florida. Americans of Cuban descent
organized the boat lift. In April alone, seven thousand, six hundred
sixty-five Cuban refugees crossed the Straits of Florida and arrived in
Key West.

In April 1980, more than 7,500 Cuban refugees arrived
in Key West, Florida, in what was known as the Mariel boatlift.

In May, the U.S. Navy and Marine Corps came to the assistance of the Coast Guard who had the principle responsibility of securing our coast. The USS *Saipan*, USS *Boulder*, and Marines from the 1st Battalion, 8th Marine Regiment, 2nd Marine Division, based at Camp Lejeune, North Carolina, were sent to Florida. President Castro had ordered that some Cuban prisoners and mental health patients be sent to Florida. Those Cubans needed constant vigilance.

The Navy had orders to assist, but not directly transport, the refugees on their voyage. The Marines were assigned to provide security at Trumbo Point and Truman Annex, both on the Naval Base at Key West. The greatest number of Cuban refugees arrived at Key West in May, a total of eighty-six thousand, four hundred eighty-eight—69 percent of the one hundred twenty-four thousand, seven hundred ninety-nine Cubans that arrived in South Florida between April and October 1980.

As the Pentagon point of contact for media queries dealing with military humanitarian assistance efforts, I had my work cut out for me the last few months of my Marine Corps career.

The major news outlets assigned a permanent correspondent to the Pentagon. They were constantly in front of my desk asking for the latest update on the number of refugees arriving that day. We developed a daily press release that covered most of the information the media was asking for, but there was always one or two writers who wanted to develop a different approach or "angle" for his or her report. This required me to make phone calls to Key West to obtain the additional information.

At the same time Cuban refugees were arriving in Key West, more than sixty thousand Haitian refugees were arriving in dilapidated boats, on rafts, and all manner of makeshift sailing vessels. The influx was so great, that in July President Carter established the State Department Cuba-Haitian Task Force (CHTF) to respond to the emergency. Marine LtCol Brill, the man I worked with during the PFC Garwood assignment, had retired and was selected to head the press office for the CHTF. I had a month left before retirement, but LtCol Brill requested that I be permitted to spend the final month of my career as a member of his staff. I would be assigned as a GS-12, but draw nothing but Marine Corps pay until after I retired from the Corps.

Keeping track of the almost 200,000 Cuban and Haitian refugees who arrived in the United States between April and October 1980.

The Pentagon and the Marine Corps agreed. In early July, I said goodbye to my friends at the Pentagon and reported to LtCol Brill at his office in Washington, D.C. I retired from the Marine Corps with 20 years of service on August 1, 1980. My immediate boss at the Pentagon, Army Lieutenant Colonel Dan Zink, was in charge of the retirement ceremony held at my American Legion post in Woodbridge.

I had retired from the Marine Corps following a 20-year career as a writer, editor, broadcaster, photographer, combat correspondent, public affairs officer, and Marine Corps spokesman at the Pentagon. Navy Commander Hank Bauman memorialized the final three years of my career with a massive 20" x 24" pen and ink cartoon which he presented to me on my final day in uniform.

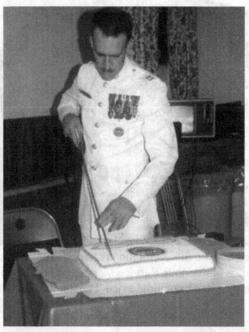

I retired from the Marine Corps following 20 years and 3 days service on August 1, 1980. The formal ceremony and retirement party was held at American Legion Post 364 in Woodbridge, Virginia.

Two months later I was summoned back to the Pentagon to receive the Defense Meritorious Service Medal. Authorized in 1977, I was the first Marine captain to be awarded the prestigious medal. At the time, it ranked third among all medals that could be awarded by the DoD.

I was called back to the Pentagon in October 1980 and presented the Defense Meritorious Service Medal, the first Marine Corps captain awarded the medal since its establishment in 1977.

CHAPTER 34

Cuban-Haitian Task Force

While every refugee's story is different and their anguish personal,
they all share a common thread of uncommon courage:
the courage not only to survive, but to persevere
and rebuild their shattered lives.

~ Antonio Guterres,
United Nations Commissioner for Refugees

The CHTF established several temporary processing facilities for the refugees. These included Fort Chaffee in Arkansas, Fort Indiantown Gap in Pennsylvania, Eglin Air Force Base in Florida, and Fort McCoy in Wisconsin. Between July and October 1980 it is estimated that the federal government spent more than two hundred thirty-three million dollars in support of CHTF operations.

Aerial view of Fort Chaffee, Arkansas, September 1980.

My job was to help LtCol Brill keep track of all the facts and figures so we could provide members of the media with constant updates as the situation unfolded. We also provided briefings for task force director Christian Holmes, and occasionally briefed members of Congress.

Carl White, a retired Marine Corps officer with whom I had served when we were both enlisted at the AFRTS on Okinawa, was in charge of the public affairs program at Fort Indiantown Gap.

The Gap, as it is often called, can trace its history to 1755 when the Pennsylvania colonial government established a string of forts in the area during the French and Indian War. The current facility was established in 1931 as a military training site for the National Guard. It was called the Edward Martin Military Reservation at the time. In 1975, it was renamed Fort Indiantown Gap. More than thirty-two thousand Vietnamese and Cambodian refugees were resettled through the nineteen-square-mile base that year.

In 1980, the Gap again became a refugee camp when over nineteen thousand Cubans were brought there for processing and sponsorship after the Mariel boatlift. White had his hands full when riots broke out there in July. At least one Cuban was killed. White gave me one of the makeshift knives fashioned from parts of a steel bed. I still have the crude knife and the custody tag describing when the knife was confiscated and who it belonged to.

Knife made from bed parts found during riots at the Cuban refugee camp at Fort Indiantown Gap, Pennsylvania, July 1980.

Fort Chaffee is located near Fort Smith in western Arkansas. It has served as an Army base, a prisoner of war facility during World War II, and on two occasions, a refugee camp. It was closed in 1995.

Fort Chaffee was a processing center for South Asian refugees in 1975 and 1976. Some fifty thousand, eight hundred and nine refugees of the Vietnam War were processed there. They received medical screenings, sponsors, and arrangements were made for their residence in the United States.

Cuban refugees from the Mariel boatlift began arriving at Fort Chaffee on May 8, 1980. In September, I went there to make photographs and document conditions at the sprawling fort.

Cuban refugees wile away the time while waiting to begin processing through the resettlement maze at Fort Chaffee.

The government was considering sending Haitians, as well as Cubans, to the Arkansas camp and Governor Bill Clinton was concerned there may be problems. There had been riots at Chaffee shortly after the first Cubans arrived and Governor Clinton was afraid they may start anew if the base population was expanded.

Three weeks after the Cubans arrived in May, some of the refugees rioted and burned two buildings. State troopers used tear gas to break up the crowd, and eighty-four Cubans were jailed. In two years, Fort

Chaffee eventually processed twenty-five thousand, three hundred ninety Cuban refugees.

Catholic nun processes a Cuban refugee at Fort Chaffee.

The refugee camp recreation director discusses
the boxing program at Fort Chaffee.

Back in Washington, D.C., the public affairs staff of the CHTF received a variety of newspapers each day. These were read carefully and all mention of the Cuban-Haitian operation was carefully clipped and passed to the task force director. The public affairs officer at each processing center did the same and sent them to our office in Washington, D.C. These were also given to the task force director.

I kept a close watch on federal job announcements during my time with the CHTF, but nothing appeared in my field. Besides, President Carter's freeze on hiring remained in effect. Waivers could be granted, such as those for the temporary Cuban-Haitian Task Force, but they were few and far between. It was election year and cutting the federal work force was a featured part of President Carter's campaign for reelection.

By October, it was evident that the CHTF was nearing an end. I was assigned to prepare the official history of our work. It would be an in-house production. Copies of the green soft cover "Report of the Cuban-Haitian Task Force," dated November 1, 1980, were given to each member of Congress, government agencies involved, and to others requesting a copy.

Cuban refugees display their artistic skills,
all available for a price, at Fort Chaffee.

Approximately one hundred twenty-five thousand Cubans had arrived in the United States' shores between May and September 1980. They came to Key West in about seventeen thousand boats.

Twenty-seven refugees died during the ninety-mile sea voyage, including fourteen on an overloaded boat that capsized on May 17, 1980.

In January 1981, the freeze on government hiring remained in effect. I learned of a photojournalism job opening at The American Legion's Washington, D.C., office. I applied and was accepted. Work at the CHTF was winding down and my leaving would not create a burden for LtCol Brill. He gave his blessing to my departure.

CHAPTER 35

The American Legion

To uphold *and defend the Constitution*
of the United States of America.
~ The American Legion Preamble, Line 2

I joined the public relations staff of the American Legion in Washington, D.C., in early February 1981. My first job was to document the annual Washington Conference at the Capitol Hilton Hotel.

The following month, Legionnaires gathered at the Washington Capitol Hilton for a national prayer breakfast, followed by a wreath laying ceremony at the Tomb of the Unknown Soldier at Arlington Cemetery where National Commander Michael Kogutek presented the American Legion's Distinguished Service Medal in memory of the dead and missing Vietnam veterans.

Following the ceremony at Arlington Cemetery we went to the White House. As we entered the Oval Office, President Ronald Reagan met us at the doorway. I was there as the Legion photographer. The Gipper shook our hand and directed us to couches and chairs that awaited our visit. The entourage included National Commander Kogutek, two future national commanders—Bruce Thiesen and Joe Frank, "CHiPS" star Larry Wilcox, and four other Vietnam-era Legionnaires.

Moving into position to make photo of President Ronald Reagan
meeting with Legionnaires to discuss the POW-MIA
issue in the Oval Office, March 16, 1981.
Photo by Jack Kightlinger, courtesy of the Ronald Reagan Library

In position.
Photo by Jack Kightlinger, courtesy of the Ronald Reagan Library

Frank, a disabled veteran in a wheelchair and I positioned ourselves in front of the president's desk, facing President Reagan and the national commander sitting at the west side of the office. The Legionnaires urged the president not to turn his back on the POW-MIA issue. President Reagan assured us he would not.

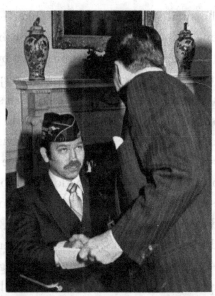

President Reagan greets Legionnaire Joe Frank of Missouri.

Two weeks to the day later President Reagan was the target of an assassination attempt as he left the Washington Hilton following a speaking engagement. Three others in his party were also shot and wounded. President Reagan's condition was "touch and go" for a while following emergency surgery, but he walked out of the George Washington University Hospital on April 11 and returned to work at the White House three days later. The following year, the shooter, John Hinckley Jr., was found not guilty by reason of insanity and committed to St. Elizabeth Hospital in Washington, D.C. He remained there until 2016 when he was released to the custody and care of his mother in Williamsburg, Virginia.

On May 13, 1981, Turk Mehmet Ali Agca attempted to assassinate Pope John Paul II at St. Peter's Square at Vatican City. Pope Paul was hit by three bullets, suffered severe blood loss, but lived. Pope Paul later forgave Agca and in June 2000, he was pardoned and deported to Turkey. With two failed assassination attempts of world leaders in a three-month period, 1981 will forever be known as the year of the would-be assassin.

A front burner issue for The American Legion in 1981 was the Vietnam Memorial, later known simply as "The Wall." Without even knowing what the final design would look like, Legionnaires had pledged to raise one million dollars to help pay for the memorial.

The National Vietnam Memorial was proposed by Jan Scruggs, an Army veteran of the Vietnam War. His idea was accepted in 1979. The Vietnam Veterans Memorial Fund was established that same year. Its goal was to raise an estimated six million dollars to build the memorial. In 1980, Congress authorized a three-acre site along Constitution Avenue.

By December of that year, more than twenty-five thousand people had paid the twenty dollar fee to enter a national competition funded by Texas millionaire and philanthropist H. Ross Perot's one hundred sixty thousand dollar donation. When the March 31, 1981, deadline arrived, fourteen hundred forty-one people had actually entered.

On March 14, 1981, Vietnam veterans and Legionnaires Junior Wyatt and Kim Splain said goodbye to Jacksonville, Illinois, and began an eight hundred eighteen-mile walk to Washington, D.C. Their goal was to call attention to the planned Vietnam Memorial and to encourage donations for its construction.

Paul Egan, of the Legion's legislative staff, and I drove to Parkersburg, West Virginia, where we met the walkers at American Legion Post 15, the halfway point of their long march. Then we returned to Washington, D.C., by way of U.S. Route 50. On our return, we stopped at each Legion post along the way to encourage the members to welcome the walkers as they passed by—a meal and refreshments would also be appreciated, along with pledges of donations to their project.

Egan and I were waiting for Splain and Wyatt when they reached the south side of the Memorial Bridge at the edge of Arlington National Cemetery to begin their final walk into the District of Columbia— past the Lincoln Memorial and on to the site chosen for the Vietnam Memorial in Constitution Gardens adjacent to the National Mall.

April 27, 1981, was groundbreaking day. The two Illinois Legionnaires had a check for thirty-five hundred dollars to hand over to Scruggs. Legionnaires of Jacksonville Post 279 eventually donated six thousand, six hundred seventy-four dollars and fifty-eight cents to the Vietnam Memorial Fund.

The panel of judges for the design competition chose an entry submitted by Maya Ying Lin, a twenty-one-year-old Yale University architect student. She received a prize of fifty thousand dollars donated by Perot. A model of her design was unveiled on May, 6, 1981, at the American Red Cross headquarters in Washington, D.C.

The Wall as it appears today with the added "Soldiers" statue overlooking the black granite wall.

The design called for a black granite memorial containing the name of every service member killed in Vietnam. It would be shaped like a wide V with one side of the V pointing to the Washington Monument. The other end would point to the Lincoln Memorial. The top of the memorial would be at ground level. Visitors would walk down a gradually sloping incline to reach the center of the V and on up the other sloping side to read all fifty-eight thousand, one hundred ninety-five of the names on the original memorial.

An aerial view of the National Vietnam Memorial in Washington, D.C. Containing the names of more than 58,000 men and women killed in Vietnam.

The National Commander of the American Legion is seldom home during his one-year term of office. If he's not visiting posts or at his office at Legion headquarters in Indianapolis, he's in Washington, D.C., visiting with members of Congress or fulfilling a myriad of other duties.

I accompanied National Commander Kogutek as he made courtesy calls on several government officials in June 1981, including newly appointed Director of the Veterans Administrator Robert P. Nimmo, and the Administrator of the Small Business Administration Michael Cardenas.

My job as a photojournalist with the American Legion opened the door to many opportunities, from shaking hands and making photos of President Reagan in the Oval Office to photographing Vice President George H. W. Bush as he welcomed members of Boys Nation to the Rose Garden. I also covered the dedication of a replica of the Liberty Bell that the Legion placed in front of Union Train Station near the Capitol Building.

In July, the director of public affairs for the Immigration and Naturalization Service, Vernon Jervis, called and said he had a job for me. I told him I had a job. He recounted with, "Hear me out. We need you in Puerto Rico by the end of the month. We're transferring the Haitian refugees from Miami to Puerto Rico and we need a public affairs presence there. You have been highly recommended for the job. It is a GS-14 position. I need an answer in two days." With that, he hung up, leaving me with a dilemma.

I went straight to my boss, Bob Hudson, a retired Air Force colonel. He was director of public affairs in the Washington, D.C., office. Hudson reported to Bob Spanogle, executive director. I liked my job. I had been with the Legion a little over five months. I didn't want to leave, but Hudson said to give the offer serious consideration. He said he would tell Spanogle I had an offer, that I was considering it, and that he would support whatever decision I made.

Spanogle had been chosen to go to Legion headquarters in Indianapolis to assume the job of national adjutant. I had prepared the press release announcing his promotion and pending move. The Burke, Virginia, newspaper, *Connection*, had published it. Spanogle lived in Burke and appreciated the publicity. I decided he would understand and accept whatever decision I made.

CHAPTER 36

Fort Allen, Puerto Rico

When was the last time you heard news accounts
of a boatload of American refugees arriving
on the shores of another country?
~ Marco Rubio, U.S. Senator

I made my decision overnight and the following day informed the American Legion leadership that I was going to Puerto Rico. My government needed me and I could not say no. I called Jervis at the INS. He told me I needed to come to his office to be formally hired, receive a briefing on the situation in Puerto Rico, and pick up my credentials and travel orders.

Fort Allen was a former U.S. Army and later U.S. Navy base. It was located on the southern coast of Puerto Rico near the town of Ponce. It had been selected as the site for a refugee camp in 1980, but its use had been blocked by one legal injunction after another. Sanitation and environmental concerns were cited. The old World War II base had been closed for many years. The abandoned living quarters had to be treated for termites. Huge rubber tents were placed around each house and they were fumigated. The small airstrip had to be cleared and prepared for tents to house the Haitians who would be flown there from Miami where they were being housed.

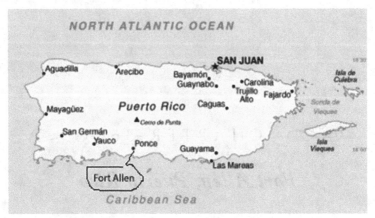

Fort Allen on the southern coast of Puerto Rico.

Haitians had been fleeing their homeland in boats for the past ten years. Many were lost at sea during the seven hundred-mile voyage from Haiti to the United States. It is estimated that more than sixty-thousand Haitians arrived in South Florida between 1977 and 1981 alone. Many of them claimed political asylum. To achieve that status they had to appear before a judge and have their cases adjudicated.

Haitian refugees congregate in the tent city erected to house them while undergoing asylum hearings at Fort Allen.

The legal delays in opening the refugee camp at Fort Allen had stirred up the citizens of Ponce and government officials in San Juan. My job would be to allay their fears by putting a positive face on what we would be doing at the camp. We would house the Haitian detainees, feed them, provide medical care when needed, process their claims for asylum, and hear their cases when they came up for review. In those days, there was no automatic path to citizenship for illegal aliens. In November 1981, claims of asylum were denied for fifty-five Haitians and the judge ordered that they immediately be flown back to Haiti. At the same time, two hundred forty-four Haitians at Fort Allen changed their minds and volunteered to return home.

Members of the U.S. Border Patrol were flown in from Arizona, New Mexico, and Texas to provide security. Judicial review judges were assigned to hear the cases. Attorneys were available to represent the Haitian detainees.

The first planeload of one hundred twenty-five Haitians arrived in Puerto Rico on August 13.

I spoke to newsmen just outside the main gate as the buses arrived. Paul La Tortue, a member of an organization seeking legal aid for Haitians, was also there. The *New York Times* reported that day:

> *This morning, in the shade of a mimosa tree outside Fort Allen, Robert L. Bowen, a spokesman for the immigration service, defended the new holding center and spoke of the amenities. "There will be TV in each compound," he said. "Soccer. Basketball. Baseball. Gloves. You name it, we've got all kinds of recreational equipment in there."*

> *In the shade of another mimosa barely five feet away, Mr. La Tortue was bellowing for all to hear: "Conditions here are worse than Krome. The heat is more intense. There is no ventilation. This is definitely worse."*

The hard work of my assignment had just begun.

A second group of Haitian refugees arrived the following day. Eventually, eight hundred Haitians would be flown from Miami to the Caribbean island. Four separate tent compounds were established at Fort Allen's old Losey Airfield.

Life at Fort Allen was pleasant for the Americans who manned the facility. I lived in the house used by the second in command when the Navy was in charge of the fort. The officer's Olympic-size swimming pool was cleaned, filled with water and available 24-7.

Major drawbacks to life at Fort Allen were the one-inch diameter holes that dotted the landscape. These were the doors to tarantula spider homes. The hairy members of the Theraphosidae family were abundant in Puerto Rico and quite unnerving for the squeamish. Then, there were massive termite nests in the trees and Indian mongooses— imported in 1877 to control the island's rat population. Mongooses were plentiful but harmless if left alone.

Fort Allen was teeming with Tarantula spiders.

No one likes to live in a tent for too long a period. To make life a little easier for the Haitians who had to live in tents, we provided them with a constant supply of native grasses and vines they could use to weave into beautiful baskets of all sizes. They were permitted to sell the traditional baskets to earn money to buy comfort items. I still have two small Haitian baskets that I purchased there.

Having accomplished my immediate task of responding to Puerto Rican concerns about what effect the Haitians would have on life in

Ponce, my job as a trained public affairs officer was nearing an end. The INS thanked me for my service and offered me permanent employment with their office in San Juan.

The job would not be as a GS-14. It called for a GS-12. This would be a serious cut in salary, plus the fact that I did not speak Spanish, the principle language on the island. So, I turned down the offer and in October returned home to search for another job.

Fort Allen remained open for another year, closing in October 1982, but the public relations crisis had been averted and I was not replaced. Tucked away in my suitcase was an old typewriter ribbon can. It contained a tarantula spider which I took home and gave to a friend for his aquarium.

CHAPTER 37

Another Job Search—Voice of America

If it's your job to eat a frog,
it's best to do it first thing in the morning.
And if it's your job to eat two frogs,
it's best to eat the biggest one first.

~ Mark Twain

As expected, having left the American Legion on such short notice just four months earlier had a chilling effect and the Legion had no job for me. So, over the next two years I bounced around from one temporary job to another in search of permanent employment. I worked as an announcer for a "Beltway bandit" making training programs for the U.S. Army, as a warehouse manager for a large furniture store, and as an employment specialist for Snelling & Snelling.

Why was it so easy to find jobs for my clients and so difficult to find employment in my career field? I can still hear the reasons for not being chosen for jobs for which I was fully qualified: "Over qualified, but no college degree" was often cited. Other reasons focused on my experience being greater than the man or woman I would work for if selected for the job.

Throughout this period, work continued on the Vietnam Veterans Memorial. The project was not without controversy. There were those who thought the design was brilliant. Others said it was not fitting for a memorial to those killed in a war. Some veterans described it as a

273

"gash in the ground," or a "pit of shame." Maya Ying Lin, the winning designer, said the memorial was for "those who have died, and for us to remember." She described it as a place for healing.

The Vietnam Memorial was dedicated on Veterans Day, November 13, 1982. There was a parade down Constitution Avenue to the site of the Memorial at Constitution Gardens. Two days earlier, on November 11th, the original day set aside for Veterans Day (before Congress chose to designate the Monday nearest the 11th as Veterans Day to give government workers a three-day weekend), the names of all those on the wall were read in a candle-lit chapel next to the National Cathedral.

Legionnaires line up on Constitution Avenue at the start of the parade commemorating the dedication of the National Vietnam Memorial, November 13, 1982.

Butch Miller, an American Legion associate, worked at the Veterans Administration. He obtained two lists, each containing twenty-five names. He read one list. I read the other. Neither of us knew any of those whose names we read that night. But, they were our brothers. We had shared a common experience, save one. They had not survived the war. We did.

All fifty-eight thousand, one hundred ninety-five names inscribed on the Vietnam Memorial initially were read that day and on into the night. President Reagan visited the chapel and listened for a while as the names were read. (Additional names were added as they became verified and in 2013, there were fifty-eight thousand, two hundred eighty-six names on the wall.) In 1998–1999, Miller served as national commander of the American Legion. I served as national vice commander in 1996–1997.

While attending the annual Marine Corps Combat Correspondents Association convention in New Orleans in August 1983, I told an old friend, Frank Beardsley, of my search for employment. He and I had been stationed together at AFRTS Okinawa and later at *Leatherneck* Magazine. Plus, we had been fishing buddies in the mid-1960s.

Beardsley was then the Director of the Special English Branch at the Voice of America in Washington, D.C. He said his office had some openings coming up, but that I would have to be tested to see if I had the ability to write in simple terms by using a limited vocabulary. The following week I took the test. I passed, and in November 1983 I was hired as a GS-12 writer-editor.

The VOA broadcasts in forty-three languages to an estimated audience of one hundred twenty-three million people "to promote freedom and democracy" around the world. When VOA was established in 1942, it was part of the Office of War Information. Today, it is the broadcast arm of the United States Information Agency. When VOA celebrated its 50th anniversary in 1992, I was successful in getting the American Legion to present the VOA a plaque recognizing its longevity achievement.

For thirteen years, I worked in VOA's Special English Branch. We worked a straight eight-hour shift because the broadcast schedule we maintained did not permit a regular lunch hour. Most of us brought a sandwich to work and ate it at our desk. At some point during my employment I got permission to keep a small three-cubic-foot refrigerator under my desk. I could now bring in sodas, condiments, cheese, and sliced meats and make my own sandwiches. I let others in the office use the refrigerator as well.

A portion of the editorial staff of the Voice of America Special English Branch
(l-r): Paul Thompson, Matt Schneider, Frank Beardsley (branch chief),
the author, Jack Huizenga, and Adam Gallan.
Beardsley, Thompson, and the author also served together
at AFRTS, Okinawa, and as combat correspondents
in Vietnam for *Leatherneck* Magazine.

Our workweek was either Sunday through Thursday or Tuesday through Saturday. I preferred Sunday through Thursday because it gave me Fridays and Saturdays off—two days that were heavy with American Legion activities in Virginia and at the national level. I was still very active at all levels of the world's largest veterans service organization. After serving as post commander in 1979–1980, I served as Virginia state membership chairman in 1988–1989 and 1989–1990, sixteenth district vice-commander in 1990–1991, and Virginia state commander in 1991–1992.

On February 17, 1988, a group of Hezbollah Guerrilla fighters kidnapped Marine Lieutenant Colonel William R. "Rich" Higgins in southern Lebanon. LtCol Higgins was a member of the United Nations Observer Group. His permanent residence in the United States was a stone's throw from my American Legion post in Woodbridge, Virginia. His name was on a list of potential members we had developed for recruiting purposes.

When a few months had gone by and nothing was heard about the fate of LtCol Higgins, I drafted a resolution for our post, calling on the Hezbollah to release LtCol Higgins. We sent a copy of the resolution to the Prince William County government. The board of county supervisors rewrote the final resolve clause, issued it as a county resolution, and forwarded it to the Virginia General Assembly. Another modification to the final resolve clause and the Commonwealth of Virginia's official call for the release of LtCol Higgins was sent to the White House.

The White House reworded the final clause, prepared the resolution for President Reagan's signature, and sent it to the United Nations Security Council. The UNSC adopted it as Resolution 618, demanding that LtCol Higgins be released immediately. The process—from beginning to end—was a text book example of a grassroots effort reaching the highest levels of government. Unfortunately, effort was for naught.

Eighteen months after LtCol Higgins was abducted, a video tape of his hanging was broadcast around the world. The date of death has never been revealed, but he was posthumously promoted to colonel and declared dead on July 6, 1990. On December 23, 1991, Col Rich Higgins' remains were recovered by a Royal Danish Army officer. He was interred at the National Cemetery in Quantico one week later, on December 30. I took a day off and attended the funeral.

Marine Colonel Rich Higgins was captured in Lebanon and brutally killed by his Hezbollah guerrilla captors, July 6, 1990.

On March 18, 1989, I was at the White House as President George H. W. Bush spoke from the South portico and elevated the Veterans Administration to a cabinet-level position. "There is only one place for the veterans of America," President Bush told those gathered on the wet White House lawn, "in the Cabinet Room, at the table with the President of the United States of America."

In 1991, I was inducted into the Army, Navy, Air Force Veterans in Canada, U.S. Unit. The ceremony was conducted during the Legion's

National Convention, held that year in Phoenix, Arizona. Nationally, I had an appointment to the Legion's Foreign Relations Commission. Today, I serve as a member of the National Legislative Counsel. I am a charter member of the Citizens Flag Alliance.

My primary job in VOA's Special English Branch was to write news or edit news written by other writers for our regular newscasts. We used a special fifteen hundred-word dictionary designed to help our foreign audience learn English and keep them informed of major news events at the same time. I also wrote a weekly agriculture report and an occasional feature for the weekly programs, "This is America," or "Science in the News."

"This is America" features I am particularly proud of include "The Alamo," "The Super Bowl," "Memorial Day," the "National Arboretum," and "Flag Day." One particular science report stands out above the rest. It described a new invention for milking mice. The device used eight silicon rubber molded teat cups. The average mouse produces one and a half milliliters of milk each day. That's less than a quarter teaspoon. Mouse milk is used in studies of mammary cancer and to make fine penetrating oil to lubricate cables and bolts. I found it hard to write the story with a straight face, and was difficult for the announcer to get through without laughing.

In 1995, I was appointed vice chairman of the American Legion's National Foreign Relation Commission. Among my many duties was to read the resolutions proposed by the Foreign Relations Convention Committee to the delegates to solicit their approval.

CHAPTER 38

Retirement

I didn't know that painters and writers retired.
They're like soldiers—they just fade away.
~ Lawrence Ferlinghetti, American Poet and Painter

I retired from VOA in January 1996. I turned fifty-five on the 12th of that month and I figured I had worked enough. By combining my twenty years of Marine Corps service and overseas combat time with my civilian government employment, I had about thirty-five years of federal employment upon which to calculate my retired pay. Our house was paid for and the monthly retired pay would be enough to support me and my wife, who had retired from the federal government the year before.

In August of 1996, I was elected national vice commander of the American Legion at our National Convention in Salt Lake City. Each year, five Legionnaires are elected to assist the national commander. My primary role was to oversee membership activities in Virginia, the District of Columbia, Maryland, Delaware, West Virginia, Ohio, Indiana, Illinois, Michigan, and the overseas department of France. The area comprised more than seven hundred thousand Legionnaires.

National Vice Commander, the American Legion, 1996–1997.

National Commander Joe Frank was the same paralyzed Vietnam vet I had sat beside in the Oval office when a group of Legionnaires met with President Reagan in March 1981. Whenever a special assignment came up in Washington, D.C., Frank would call. I represented the Legion at the White House and at Arlington National Cemetery on Veterans Day 1996 and on Memorial Day 1997. I accompanied the national commander to the White House in July 1997 when President Bill Clinton announced his support for the expansion of NATO by adding Hungary, Poland, and the Czech Republic.

Representing the American Legion and meeting President Bill Clinton
at the White House on Veterans Day, 1996.

I represented the American Legion during graduation at the Naval Academy in 1997, and at the christening ceremony for the USS *Cook* (DDG-75) a guided missile destroyer, at Bath Iron Works in Bath, Maine, on May 3, 1997. The ship was named for Marine Colonel Donald G. Cook, a Medal of Honor recipient who died in captivity as a POW during the Vietnam War.

Two years later, the Navy christened and launched DDG-76, named in honor of another Marine, Col Higgins. As you've already read in this book, Col Higgins was murdered by Hezbollah guerrillas in Lebanon. The USS *Higgins* was under construction and laying alongside the USS *Cook*, when I attended the USS *Cook* christening in 1997.

At the christening of the USS *Cook* (DDG-75) in Bath Maine,
with Herm Harrington. The future USS *Higgins* (DDG-76)
is berthed alongside without hull number.

Membership retention and recruiting duties in the American Legion took me to every jurisdiction in my coverage area as national vice commander except France, at least once. Of particular note was the weeklong membership tours of Indiana and Illinois. These two tours covered the width and length of both states and produced many memories and several lifelong friendships. The dedication of a new Veterans Hospital in Wilmington, Delaware, and attendance at Boys State in Virginia and Ohio were particularly memorable.

Boys State is a weeklong program that teaches rising high school juniors how local and state governments work. Two boys from each state are selected as "senators" and sent to Washington, D.C., for Boys Nation where they learn government at the federal level. Each Boys Nation elects a president and vice president. The American Legion Auxiliary conducts a parallel program for rising junior girls at the state and national level.

In October 1998, my wife's application for membership in the Daughters of the American Revolution was approved. Membership in the DAR is not a simple process. Each link in the applicant's genealogy must be documented by birth certificates, wills, death notices, censuses, etc. The patriotic Revolutionary War service of the qualifying ancestor must be supported by pension papers or some other means.

With Helen in the DAR, it was time for me to look into the possibility being eligible for membership in the SAR—Sons of the American Revolution. It had taken several years of research to gather Helen's qualifying documentation. The computer helped, but trips to Maryland, North Carolina, and Mississippi, and several days at the DAR library in Washington, D.C., were needed to pull it all together. My search would be more difficult because I did not know if I had an ancestor who served in the Revolutionary War. What's more no one in my family—neither on my mother's side, nor my father's side—had ever done any family research. I would be plowing virgin soil.

Mom was a big help. She remembered a story from her youth about Grandpa Thompson being a drummer boy during the war. That turned out to be wrong, but Bartholomew Thompson, my mom's third great-grandfather on her mother's side, had served as a soldier in the Revolutionary War. So, that's where my research began.

For the next three years—1999, 2000, and 2001—each summer, Helen and I would drive to Norfolk, pick up Mom and continue to Stanley, North Carolina. That is where Mom was born and where three of her sisters still lived. It also was where most of her side of the family came from, dating back to the Revolutionary War and beyond.

During those three years, we visited every cemetery in the six-county area of Gaston, Catawba, Lincoln, Iredell, Cleveland, and Burke looking for the final resting place of ancestors. We visited libraries, court houses, and genealogy record repositories. I made hundreds of photographs.

My research for qualifying information for membership in the SAR proved successful in a few months, but caught up in learning about my family, I put off making formal application for SAR membership and worked on my family history. My research had turned up nineteen grandfathers on my mom's side of the family who either fought in or provided patriotic service during the Revolutionary War. The grandfather I eventually used as my primary patriotic ancestor—Robert Abernethy—was a delegate to North Carolina's Halifax Convention in 1776 when the State's Constitution was written, approved, and signed into law. Abernethy was one of the signers.

Researching my father's family resulted in several trips to Huntington, West Virginia, and nearby towns, as well as the southwest Virginia counties of Botetourt, Montgomery, Craig, Giles, and Tazewell. I identified ten grandfathers who served during the Revolutionary War on my dad's side of the family.

When I finished my family history, "Roots and Sucker Shoots—A Report of the Abernethy, Bowen and Allied Families," I dedicated it to my mom, and presented her the first copy on her 90th birthday. Her eyesight and memory had begun to fade by then, but she read the book from cover to cover with the aid of a huge magnifying glass.

One passage dealt with the fact that my Grandpa Hugha Bowen had two wives; each of them bearing him eleven children. Hugha sired his last child—my great grandfather, Alderson Bowen—when he was seventy-six-years old. "And that was before Viagra," I wrote. Some ladies from Mom's church visited her one day and she recounted the prowess of Grandpa Hugha. When she reached the punch line, she blurted out, "and that was before Vigoro!" The ladies were still chuckling when they departed several hours later.

CHAPTER 39

September 11, 2001

Time is passing. Yet, for the United States of America,
there will be no forgetting September the 11ᵗʰ.
We will remember every rescuer who died in honor.
We will remember every family that lives in grief.
We will remember the fire and ash, the last phone calls,
the funerals of the children.

~ President George W. Bush,
43rd President of the United States

Each year following the American Legion National Convention, the newly elected national commander travels to Washington, D.C., to brief a joint session of the House and Senate Veterans Affairs Committees on resolutions passed by the delegates at the convention. I have attended these sessions since the 1980s.

In 2001, Legionnaires gathered in Washington, D.C., on September 11 for the national commander's testimony. The time was 9:00 a.m. We had just completed breakfast at the Rayburn House Office Building. We were moving to the Cannon House Office Building for the briefing session when we noticed that everyone one we passed was talking frantically on their cell phone and looking at the sky. That day will forever be known as 9/11.

The first hijacked plane, American Airlines Flight 11, had crashed into the north tower of the World Trade Center fourteen minutes earlier at 8:46. At 9:03 a.m., United Airlines Flight 175 crashed into the south tower. Finding themselves trapped by the raging fire that followed the two explosions, as many as two hundred fifty people jumped to their deaths.

The World Trade Center on 9/11, before the buildings collapsed.
Photo courtesy of Michael Foran, © 2001 Michael Foran

Rumors were rampant in Washington, D.C., when it became known that a third and later a fourth passenger plane had been hijacked. Where were those planes headed? The Capitol was a logical target and everyone in that huge building raced to get as far away as possible. There were a lot of bruises, scrapes, and cuts as senators, representatives, congressional staffers, and tourists tripped and fell rushing down the marble and granite steps in the interior and exterior of the building.

The Legionnaires who had come to Washington, D.C., to hear National Commander Ric Santos testify quickly moved to a vacant hearing room in the Cannon House Office Building. National Adjutant Bob Spanogle provided regular updates.

I was sitting next to a window on the west side of the hearing room when the muffled sound of an explosion reverberated through the room. The time was 9:37 a.m., American Airlines Flight 77 had just crashed into the western side of the Pentagon, less than five miles away. The crash claimed the lives of one hundred eighty-four innocent victims—one hundred twenty-five in the Pentagon and fifty-nine on the plane—as well as five Al-Qaeda hijackers.

The Pentagon, where 184 innocent people died on 9/11,
plus five Al-Qaeda hijackers.

The death toll for the two World Trade Center towers, including passengers on the planes, workers in the building, and firemen, police, and other first responders, was two thousand, seven hundred forty-nine plus five hijackers on each plane. Both buildings collapsed while millions watched "live" television coverage of the unfolding tragedy. Fires at Ground Zero burned for more than ninety days.

Twenty-six minutes after Flight 77 slammed into the Pentagon, passengers onboard United Airlines Flight 93 took matters into their own hands and attempted to subdue the four Al-Qaeda hijackers on that plane. "Are you guys ready?" passenger Todd Beamer said, "Let's roll!"

The plan to subdue the hijackers resulted in bringing the plane crashing to the ground. It tore into a field near Shanksville, Pennsylvania. All forty passengers and crew members onboard were killed, as well as the four hijackers. It is believed the terrorists had intended to crash the plane into either the Capitol or the White House in Washington, D.C.

When word of the fourth plane crash reached the Legionnaires in the Cannon House Office Building, we began an orderly move from the east side of the Capitol, west on C Street to 1st Street, SW, where we turned north to Constitution Avenue, east to New Jersey, and north to the Hyatt Regency Hotel where we were staying. When we arrived, Legionnaires from Michigan were gathered at the front of the hotel. They had used a different route. Senator Debbie Stabenow (D-MI) was with them. She attended our breakfast that morning at the Rayburn House Office Building. She stayed with her Legionnaire constituents until after the all-clear was sounded.

I had driven to Washington, D.C., that morning and left my car at an underground PMI parking garage. Not anticipating a need for my cell phone, I had left it in the car. My wife, Helen, had no way to get in touch with me and she was frantic with worry. Not only was I on Capitol Hill, but her daughter, Brenda, an IT supervisor for the Army at nearby Crystal City, frequently had meetings at the Pentagon. Helen was unable to get in touch with her.

I left the Hyatt at about 2:00 p.m. When I reached my car I called and briefed Helen on what had transpired. The drive home was surprisingly smooth. Fire and smoke still billowed out of the Pentagon as I drove by on Route 395. At every overhead walkway and road I drove under heading south, an American flag was waving proudly in the breeze. I was witnessing the first of a national outpouring of patriotic enthusiasm that continued unabated for several years. It was also the first time the American Legion national commander had not testified before Congress.

CHAPTER 40

Flag Protection Amendment

The Congress shall have power to prohibit the
physical desecration of the flag of the United States.
~ Proposed Amendment to the United States Constitution

During the latter years of the 1980s, the 1990s in their entirety, and the first six years of the new millennium, I was almost constantly on the road going to and from flag protection programs throughout Virginia, in Washington, D.C., and at Legion Headquarters in Indianapolis, Indiana.

The flag protection issue surfaced when Gregory Johnson burned an American flag during the Republican National Convention in Dallas in 1984. He was arrested, charged, and found guilty of violating a federal statute specifically prohibiting flag desecration, but a Texas Appeals Court overturned the conviction on the grounds that burning the flag was protected speech under the First Amendment of the U.S. Constitution.

The case eventually reached the Supreme Court, where the Appeals Court decision was upheld. Congress quickly rewrote the federal law in 1989, but it too was struck down by the Supreme Court the following year.

That's when the American Legion said "enough's enough" and weighed in with its three million members in support of efforts to protect the flag Legionnaires had served in the military to defend.

289

Their initial effort was to gather grassroots support for their "save the flag program." To reach their goal they focused first on the state legislatures. Each state legislative body was asked to pass a memorializing resolution calling on Congress to protect Old Glory from physical desecration. Virginia was the thirty-second state to climb onboard for this effort in 1992, while I was serving as state commander of the American Legion.

The author and CFA President Dan Wheeler prior to a press conference on the capitol grounds in Richmond, Virginia.

In 1994, the American Legion founded the Citizens Flag Alliance, a group of community, civic, veterans, patriotic, and like-minded organizations whose one objective was to win passage of a congressional amendment to protect the American Flag from physical desecration. I was present at Legion Headquarters in Indianapolis when the CFA was established and became a charter member. Today, the CFA has more than one hundred forty members, including the SAR and the Marine Corps Combat Correspondents Association.

Legionnaires from around the country gathered in Washington, D.C.,
on several occasions to demonstrate their support
for flag protection legislation.
Photo courtesy of *The American Legion* Magazine.

The first flag protection legislation offered in the House and Senate in June 1990 had been defeated. In 1992, President Bill Clinton told delegates to the American Legion National Convention meeting in Chicago that he opposed flag burning, but when new legislation was introduced in both houses of Congress in 1995, a White House representative testified before the Senate Judiciary Committee and said President Clinton opposed the flag amendment.

From that point forward, every time the proposed flag amendment came up for a judicial committee hearing or floor vote in either the House or Senate, I was there. There were a lot of spirit-lifting moments when the measure would get a positive vote in committee and when the House voted to approve. The Senate was always the stickler.

In January 1997, I had a chance encounter with Michigan Congressman Dale Kildee. We were both at Washington National (now Reagan) Airport awaiting a flight to Michigan. He was going home to meet with his constituents. I was on my way to Swartz

Creek for a Michigan state Legion membership meeting. I was a national vice commander at the time. Michigan one of my states of responsibility.

Congressman Kildee spoke first. He had noticed the Legion emblem on the windbreaker I was wearing. He had attended American Legion Boys State in Michigan in his youth and had won his first political election during the weeklong program he attended. We chatted about the Boys State program for a while, then I shifted to the flag amendment.

I knew the voting position of every senator and congressman/woman in the states in my coverage area as a national vice commander. Congressman Kildee was not a supporter. I asked "why not?" He replied, "Tell me why I should be." So I did. I quoted the statistics, the positive surveys in support, the fact that the measure had passed the House every time it was voted on despite his and others' opposition, and I quoted Major General Patrick Brady's favorite line, besides, "it's the right thing to do." Congressman Kildee said I'd given him something to think about. Our flight was called. He went to first class. I went to coach.

I didn't see Congressman Kildee again until the day of the next vote. And then, it was an overhead view from my seat in the House gallery when the next Flag Amendment came up for a vote on June 12, 1997. I must admit my chest puffed a tad when the green light beside Congressman Kildee's name lit up on the huge tote board that's projected above the speaker's dais during all house votes—indicating his affirmative vote.

My biggest surprise came that night after I returned home. The phone rang about 8:30 p.m. Congressman Kildee was on the phone. "I just wanted you to know you were most convincing when we met at the airport earlier this year. I vote YEA for the flag amendment today." All I could say was "I know, congressman, I was there. And, I thank you."

CFA President Dan Wheeler celebrates the House
Passage of the Flag Amendment, June 12, 1997.
The author communicates the good news to his
state headquarters in Richmond, VA.

Despite survey after survey of the American people showing that flag protection was favored by 75–80 percent of the population and that burning the flag and other forms of desecration were not considered free speech issues, the Senators rejected every measure that came before them.

Several senators changed their minds along the way. Chuck Robb of Virginia, Mitch McConnell of Kentucky, Richard Bryan of New Mexico, and Robert Byrd of West Virginia were among those who were "for it before they were against it."

Waiting Game—Legionnaires visit Senator Mitch McConnell's
office as the amendment vote approaches. Much to
their chagrin, the senator declined to meet with them.
Photo courtesy of *The American Legion* Magazine.

The final vote on the issue came in the Senate on June 26, 2006. The House had passed identical legislation on June 22 the previous year by a winning margin of 286–130. The American Legion and CFA had gone "all out" during the intervening months to gather support. Several "Walk the Hill" events were organized by the CFA for its members to meet with objecting or "on the fence" senators. SAR President General Roland Downing attended one such effort, joining with CFA Chairman and Medal of Honor recipient MajGen Brady and CFA President Dan Wheeler.

CFA President Dan Wheeler, SAR President General Roland Downing, and CFA Board Chairman Pat Brady, a Medal of Honor recipient and retired army major general, hold a strategy session before walking the halls of Congress to meet with senators who have not yet committed to voting for the flag amendment.

Despite this all-out effort, the Flag Amendment failed once more in the Senate. This time by one vote, 66–34. The Flag Amendment continues to be a legislative priority of the American Legion, but it has not been voted on since 2006.

The American Legion has never been a single issue organization. While fighting for Congress to support flag protection legislation, the Legion helped raise funds for the Vietnam War Memorial, the Korean War Memorial, the Military Nurses Memorial, the World War II Memorial, and the Women in Military Service for America Memorial. My wife and I attended all five ground breakings and dedications.

President Bill Clinton, Senator Bob Dole, and actor Tom Hanks
were among the dignitaries who wielded a shovel during the
groundbreaking ceremony for the World War II Memorial
on Veterans Day, November 11, 2000.

The author and his wife, Helen, brushed aside the sweltering heat
to attend the dedication of the World War II Memorial on May 29, 2004.

The cry from the Citizens Flag Alliance was and continues to
be "Let the People Decide." But, the principal goal of the American
Legion as 2016 came to an end was the nation's veterans. That's the
way it was when the American Legion was founded in 1919 and despite

vast improvements in veterans' care over the years, recent revelations about waiting times at Veterans Administration hospitals have resulted in a refocusing of the Legion effort.

Lurking in the background, the effort to protect Old Glory remains a top priority. Each year, sponsors for the legislation are sought out. It's introduced in both houses of Congress, but once there, it languishes for lack of attention. A new Congress, the 115th, will begin its two-year term in January 2017. Newly elected congressmen/women and senators will begin their work for the first time. The slate will be wiped clean of pending legislation and, along the way, someone will introduce legislation to protect Old Glory from physical desecration.

Why, after twenty-seven years of steady disappointment do we continue our efforts to protect the flag? MajGen Brady still answers that question best: "It's the right thing to do."

CHAPTER 41

Sons of the American Revolution

The liberties of our country, the freedom of our civil constitution, are worth defending at all hazards . . . We have received them as a fair inheritance from our worthy ancestors . . . (they) transmitted them to us with care and diligence.
~ Samuel Adams, American Statesman and Founder

My application for membership in the National Society of the Sons of the American Revolution was approved in August 2000 and I was inducted into Virginia's Colonel Fielding Lewis Chapter the following month. Three years later I was elected chapter president. The highlight of my term in office was presenting a bronze plaque to the Fredericksburg Museum in recognition of the town's 275th anniversary.

The man who wears this insignia is a proud member of the
National Society of the Sons of the American Revolution.
He had an ancestor who fought or provided patriotic service
to help gain our freedom during the Revolutionary War.

I transferred my membership from the chapter in Fredericksburg to the Culpeper Minute Men Chapter in 2006. Four members of the Fielding Lewis Chapter were elected state officers that year and I didn't feel comfortable with one chapter having 40 percent of the state officers. The state had twenty-six chapters.

The National Society of the SAR was founded in 1889 and chartered by Congress in 1906. Female descendants of Revolutionary War soldiers and patriots established the Daughters of the American Revolution in 1890. By 2016, the DAR had admitted more than nine hundred fifty thousand members into its organization.

The SAR is the largest male lineage organization in the United States. It has fifty state societies, with more than five hundred local chapters, and several international societies have more than thirty-four thousand members. The SAR is dedicated to assisting its members, schools, teachers, and the general public preserve the history of the United States, its constitutional principles, and the men and women who fought and provided patriotic service to help gain our freedom. U.S., co

Its members come from every walk of life including military officers, judges, business leaders, doctors, kings, princes, governors, senators, and presidents of the United States. Spain's King Juan Carlos is a member based on his ancestor's financial assistance to General Washington during the war. British Prime Minister Winston Churchill was also a member, based on his mother's ancestors.

American Presidents Ulysses S. Grant, Rutherford B. Hayes, Benjamin Harrison, William McKinley, Theodore Roosevelt, William H. Taft, Warren G. Harding, Calvin Coolidge, Herbert C. Hoover, Franklin Roosevelt, Harry S. Truman, Dwight D. Eisenhower, Lyndon B. Johnson, Gerald R. Ford, Jimmy Carter, George H. W. Bush, and George W. Bush were, or are, members of the SAR.

I began working at the national level of the SAR even before being elected to any office at the chapter or state levels. I attended an Atlantic District Meeting in New Jersey in August 2001, and newly elected President General Larry McClanahan of Tennessee, appointed me a member of the National Flag Committee. The following month,

I attended my first National Trustees Meeting at SAR headquarters in Louisville, Kentucky.

My wife and I attended our first Annual Congress (equivalent of a national convention) in Nashville, Tennessee in 2002. Between then and 2013 when my wife's health began interfering with SAR activities, we attended eleven annual meetings and twenty-three National Trustee gatherings.

"Walking the Walk" with Helen and being introduced as Historian General of the SAR in Phoenix, Arizona, July 2012.

Along the way, we attended numerous patriot grave markings and commemorative programs, including those at King's Mountain, Guilford Courthouse, Moore's Creek Landing, and Ramsour's Mill in North Carolina; Cowpens, Buford's Massacre, and Hanging Rock in South Carolina; Petersburg, Yorktown, Green Springs, Battle of Cape Henry, the Blockhouse, and Martin Station in Virginia; Kettle Creek in Georgia; Fort Laurens in Ohio; Fort Henry and Point Pleasant in West Virginia, Vincennes and Massacre of Colonel De La Balme in Indiana;

Lookout Mountain and Sycamore Shoals in Tennessee; Blue Licks in Kentucky; and Arkansas Post in Arkansas.

In 2007, I was elected vice president general for the International District. The following year, my wife and I visited Scotland and England with a delegation of SAR members headed by President General Bruce Wilcox. While there, we dedicated a plaque and presented a wreath at the birthplace of Captain John Paul Jones. We also presented a wreath at Flamborough Head overlooking the site of the Revolutionary War battle between Captain Jones, in the *Bonhomme Richard*, and the British man-of-war, *Serapis*.

While in Scotland, we visited Ayrshire, the birthplace of poet Robert Burns; the town of Dumfries, the place Burns is buried; the castles of Edinburgh, Sterling, Uquhart, White, and York; the smallest distillery of Scotch whiskey, Edradour; and Loch Ness, home of Nessie. We even found time to attend a traditional Scottish night of singing, and enjoyed a taste of haggis.

Gateway to Scotland, entering from England.
The other side of the boulder welcomes
you to England.

During the waning days of our whirlwind visit, we traveled to the northern Highlands to see where the Battle of Culloden took place. We placed another wreath there in memory of General Hugh Mercer. He took part in his first battle there in 1746 while serving as a surgeon in the Jacobite Army led by Bonnie Prince Charlie.

The huge burial cairn monument at Culloden marking the spot where as many as 2,000 Jacobites were killed in 1746. Hugh Mercer, a future George Washington general officer during the American Revolution, was there as a surgeon. He escaped the slaughter and fled to America.

The Jacobites, consisting mainly of Scots, were soundly defeated at Culloden, losing between fifteen hundred and two thousand men killed or wounded. Gen Mercer fled to the United States. He joined George Washington in his colonial battles and later as a general in the Revolutionary War.

Gen Mercer is the only American general officer ever to die in battle after being wounded by a bayonet. This occurred during the Battle of Princeton in 1777. He had settled in Fredericksburg, Virginia, and opened an apothecary shop. The Fielding Lewis Chapter of the SAR joins with the local Fredericksburg Scottish Society to commemorate his life there each year.

Presenting wreath during Battle Days in 2008,
commemorating the Battle of Point Pleasant,
as a vice president general of the SAR.

In 2003, I was named to head a special committee to commemorate the 225th anniversary of the many battles of the Revolutionary War. We were eight years late beginning our program, but during the life of the committee, The Revolutionary War (225th Anniversary) Committee commemorated more than twenty battles and events, beginning with the Battle of Kettle Creek in 1779 in Georgia and ending with the Battle of Arkansas Post, the LAST battle of the Revolutionary War in 1783.

I photographed and reported on each of the programs in more than fifteen states, traveling the equivalent of two and one-half times around the world . . . in my car. The program came to an end in September 2012 with a gala program in Philadelphia to observe the 225th anniversary of the signing of the U.S. Constitution.

In 2010, I was elected president of the Virginia Society. Virginia won its 10th straight Admiral Furlong Award that year for its participation in the SAR Flag Certificate Program. I had established the program in Virginia in 2001 when I was appointed state flag chairman. When I was elected state secretary three years later, Dr. Kirk Sheap assumed the chairmanship. When this book went to the publisher in 2016, Sheap was still flag chairman and Virginia still had its unbroken string of annual Admiral Furlong Award recognition intact.

Leading the parade down Main Street during the 2010 program
commemorating the American victory at Yorktown
as President of the Virginia Society of the SAR.

I was elected historian general of the national society in 2012 at its Annual Congress in Phoenix. Six months later, my active involvement in the society came to an end when my wife was diagnosed with Alzheimer's. I had been awarded a number of awards along with way, including the state-and national-level Distinguished Service Medal, each level of the Meritorious Service Medal, and the Minuteman Medal, the highest recognition a member of the SAR can receive.

Formal campaign photo for the office of historian general.

I continue to report on the annual visit of the SAR president general to the National Convention of the American Legion in the fall issue of *The SAR Magazine*. I established the program in 2003. The president general of the world's largest male lineal society brings greetings to the world's largest veterans organization and presents the outgoing national commander a framed Certificate of Patriotic Service. The national commander is invited to attend the SAR Annual Congress each year.

 PHOTOS BY THE AUTHOR

First Marine Division Informational Services Office

Marine Combat Correspondents assigned to the 1st MarDiv ISO were a motley crew. Capt Mawk Arnold was the officer in charge, but the enlisted staff of E-5s and below—the Snuffies—were led by Sgt Dale "Daddy" Dye. It was, perhaps, the greatest gathering of writers and broadcasters ever assembled in one office for the purpose of reporting on a war, in this case, the Vietnam War. Members of the shop with whom I still communicate include Mawk Arnold, Dale Dye, Rick Lavers, Dale Hunter, Bob Bayer, Mike Stokey, and Chuck Lane.

A rare gathering of the First Marine Division ISO for a beer party at China Beach near Da Nang, August 1968. Standing (l-r): Eric Grimm, Gary Clark, the author, Hal Blake, Woodrow Cheeley, Bob Bayer, Frank Wiley, Dale Hunter, Dick Licciardi, Tim Godfrey, Jerry Goodall, Art Kybat, Jim Hardy, Daven Morey. Kneeling (l-r): Larry LePage, Chuck Lane, Jim Glover, Mawk Arnold, Dale Dye, Larry Saski, Don Wilkerson, and Bob Rea.

Celebrating the Marine Corps Birthday, November 10, 1968.

Captain Arnold (center rear) visits his ISO shop to find the crew
busy writing stories about their most recent trips to the field.

Sgt Dale "Daddy" Dye, Chief Snuffie

Maj Mawk Arnold, age 92. At 2016
USMCCCA Conference
in Fredericksburg, Virginia.

Sgt Bob Bayer, writer.

SSgt Bob Bowen,
the author.

LCpl Dale Hunter,
Radio-TV.

Gunny Chuck Lane, press chief.

Sgt Rich Lavers, writer

Sgt Mike Stokey, writer

The coveted named plaque presented
to every member of the 1st MarDiv
ISO staff when they left, signifying
their membership in an elite club
of combat correspondents.

"Corpsman Up"

Navy Corpsmen saved countless lives during the Vietnam War. But, in performing their heroics on the battlefield, six hundred thirty-nine Corpsmen were killed, twenty-one of them in the same battalion, 3/26. Four Navy Corpsmen, assigned to the Marine Corps, were awarded the Medal of Honor for bravery under fire in Vietnam. When not in the field with their Marines, Corpsmen could often be found conducting medical civil affairs programs in the villages, where they were equally popular.

HN D. J. "Doc" Wiggins awaits the call for "Corpsman Up" signifying he has a wounded Marine to attend.

HM/2 Cecil W. Peterson (r) applies a Neil Robertson
sling to a wounded Marine for evacuation
by helicopter during Operation Maui Peak.

Caught in an ambush, the bullets were still flying overhead when the
Corpsman and Marine combat correspondent GySgt Lee Witconis rushed
to the aid of this wounded Marine during Operation Independence.

A twisted ankle gets attended to by a Corpsman
on patrol with 1/1 south of Da Nang.

Wounded Marine is whisked from
the battlefield in a CH-46 chopper.

Corpsman treats a young Vietnamese girl with foot
fungus during a civil affairs medical program.

Corpsman bandages the arm of a Bravo 1/1 Marine,
wounded during a river patrol south of Da Nang.

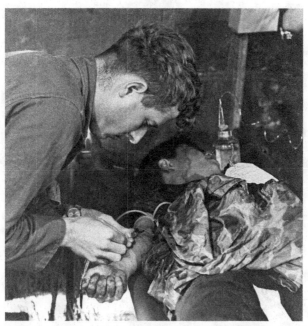
Navy Corpsman inserts an IV in the arm of a wounded North
Vietnamese soldier at field med in An Hoa, south of Da Nang.

The Grunts

They were young. They were old. They were white, black, brown, yellow, and every shade in between. They were America's finest doing America's dirty work of making war. They were Marines, soldiers, airmen, sailors, and coast guardsmen. They were the unsung heroes of the Vietnam War. The Marines called their fighting men grunts.

Beware of the water buffalo.

C-ration box coolie hat.　　　　　　On patrol.

Peeling spuds on Marble Mountain.

Cooling off period for men of Charlie 1/1.

The thousand-yard stare.

The Officers

There are three groups of military officers: company grade (second lieutenant–captain), field grade (major–colonel), and general officer grade (brigadier general–full four-star general). During combat situations, they all want a field command, be it at the platoon, company, battalion, regiment, division, or force level. A few of the better ones I had the privilege of accompanying on combat operations in Vietnam.

LtCol A. A. Laporte, CO, 1/1, checks his map coordinates beside a "watering hole" left by an artillery shell during Operation Meade River south of Da Nang.

1stLt James Huffman, CO, Bravo 1/7.

Capt Hank Trautwein, CO, Charlie 1/1.

LtCol Leon Utter, CO, 2/7.

Capt Carl Reckewell (center rear), CO, Fox 2/9.

Col Robert Laufer (l), CO First Marine Regiment
briefs MajGen Carl Youngdale on the conduct
of Operation Meade River.

LtCol Al "Red Dog" Keller, CO, 2/27.

General and Flag Officers

Marine officers in pay grades O-7—O-10 are called general officers. Navy officers in the same pay grades are called admirals or flag officers. We had our share of both with positions of responsibility during the Vietnam War. Some made their headquarters in Hawaii. Most of them were in Vietnam living alongside the grunts that fought the war up close and personal. During my time covering the war, I met and photographed many of them.

LtGen Lewis Walt, CG of III MAF and I Corps congratulates a young Marine engineer for his plans for the layout of a new mess hall at Camp Carroll.

Adm John McCain, Jr., Commander of the Pacific Command,
meets with Marines of the First Reconnaissance Battalion at their
headquarters on Hill 327 in Da Nang, 1968. McCain was the
father of Navy LtCdr John McCain II, who was shot down
and a resident of the Hanoi Hilton as a POW at the time.

BGen Jonas M. Platt, CG of Task Force Delta, receives
a field briefing during Operation Utah, March 1966.

Gen Leonard Chapman, (c) CMC, and III MAF CG, LtGen Herman Nickerson, take the general's launch after meeting with reporters at the Da Nang Press Center.

Adm Roy Johnson, Commander of the Pacific Fleet following a visit to Da Nang, 1966.

LtGen Herman Nickerson, CG, III MAF, gave visiting
Senator Barry Goldwater an aerial tour of northern I Corps, 1969.

LtGen Victor Krulak, CG, Fleet Marine Force, Pacific, received
a field briefing from Capt Carl Reckewell, CO, Fox 2/9,
south of Da Nang, February 1966.

LtGen Lewis Walt (c), CG III MAF, is flanked by MajGen Herman Nickerson (l) CG, 1st MarDiv, and MajGen Louis Robertshaw, CG, 1st Marine Air Wing, during the morning brief at Walt's headquarters in Da Nang, February 1966.

BGen James Herbold, Jr., CG of the Force Logistic Command, the Marine Corps' provider of beans, bullets, and bandages during the war.

MajGen Carl Youngdale, CG, 1st MarDiv (c), received
an update on Operation Meade River by OPCON
Col Robert Laufer (l), December 1968. Meade River
was the Marine Corps' largest helicopter operation of the war.

Da Nang Press Center and the Correspondents

Most of the news of the Vietnam War from in and around Da Nang came through the Press Center, housed in an old French villa on the Han River. All five major Marine commands: FLC, the 1st and 3rd Air Wings, and the 1st and 3rd Divisions had their own news gathering functions, but release authority rested with the III MAF Information Officer who was based at the CIB at the Da Nang Press Center. That was also where the foreign correspondents and freelance reporters slept and ate when not in the field gathering news of the war. Their work was not reviewed prior to publication. The Marine Corps went all out to assist them get their stories in the field and arrange for interviews with senior officers.

A jeep arrives at the Da Nang Press Center with a batch of photographs and news releases prepared by writers at the 1st MarDiv on Hill 327.

III MAF Information Officer Col Tom Fields discusses
an upcoming operation with AP photographer Rick Merron.

The CIB photo lab was parked right outside the room *Leatherneck*
Magazine correspondents called home when not in the field.

Gunny Charlie Ross (l) discusses an enhancement needed for a photo being printed for release by SSgt Kelley of the CIB Photo Section.

With reports filed for the day it was time for a game of 7-14-21 at the bar (l-r): freelance reporter Charlie Durden, AP correspondent Bob Gassaway, freelance reporter Tom Dell (may they all rest in peace) and the author. From the looks of the expression on my face I must have lost the dice game.

Gunny Jack Childs (l) and MSgt Walt Stewart (c) discuss escort plans
for an upcoming operation. While it was not required that
civilian reporters be escorted while in the field, the CIB offered
the service and most newsmen used an escort.

UPI photographer Tim Page focuses on a resupply of
five-gallon water cans during Operation New York while
other photographers await their turn for a good vantage point.

UPI correspondent Joe Galloway (c) caught a chopper hop to Operation Double Eagle II, February 1966. Galloway, author of the award-winning *We were Soldiers Once . . . and Young* is widely acclaimed as one of the best combat correspondents to emerge from the Vietnam War.

Award winning photographer, Eddie Adams of the AP, enjoys a soda pop break before photographing the court-ordered execution of a Chinese black marketeer in Saigon, March 1966. Two years later, Adams, a Marine photographer during the Korean War, photographed the execution of a Vietcong soldier on the streets of Saigon. That photo earned Adams the Pulitzer Prize.

UPI correspondent Bob Ibrahim, Korean War Marine, was right at home among his Marines at Da Nang.

George Esper was the AP bureau chief in Da Nang, 1966. He later moved to Saigon and served as bureau chief there. He covered the Vietnam War for more than ten years before coming home and teaching journalism at the University of West Virginia.

CBS correspondent Bruce Morton is given a briefing on Operation
Independence while CIB escorts Gunny Lee Witconis (l)
and 2ndLt Dick Arnold (r) look on.

Birdseye view of the Da Nang Press Center. The
Cultural Museum, with ancient stone statuary
can be seen in the right background.

SSgt Steve Stibbens covered the war for the
Pacific Stars & Stripes Newspaper and *Leatherneck*
Magazine before doing the same for the AP.
Photo by Horst Faas, AP.

Wally McNamee was a Marine photographer
in Korea and then for *Washington Post* in Vietnam.

Operation Double Eagle

The largest amphibious landing by the United States since the Inchon Landing in Korean in 1950. Marines hit the beach near Chu Lai in the early hours of January 28, 1966. Marines of the 1st and 4th Regiments were involved. I came ashore with Lima Company, BLT 3/1. The final situation report from Task Force Delta on February 17, listed three hundred twelve Vietcong killed, nineteen captured, and two hundred seventy-eight suspects detained. The Marines had covered five hundred square miles in those three weeks, making it their largest sustained operation of the war.

A beachmaster guides a Mike boat during amphibious landing Phase of Operation Double Eagle.

Battalion Landing Team 3/1 heads to the beach in their Mike boat.

Marines of Lima, 3/1 are briefed on the landing that they'll make the next day.

A clean weapon is the objective of every Marine . . . especially in combat.

It was overcast and drizzling when Operation Double Eagle launched, January 28, 1966.

A UH-34D helicopter flits by overhead during the landing.

Marines come ashore during Operation Double Eagle.

Marine takes up hasty fighting position as the advance inland begins.

Defending the available high ground.

Operation New York

Marine Task Unit Hotel—Companies F and G of the 2nd Battalion 1st Marines and Company K of the 3rd Battalion 1st Marines, Third Marine Division—joined with the 1st Division of the South Vietnamese Army in a combat operation near the village of Pho Lai, northwest of Hue where a large Vietcong unit was known to be. One-hundred-twenty Vietcong were killed and seven captured during the five-day operation, February 26–March 3, 1966. Seventeen Marines were killed and thirty-seven wounded.

A Marine of Fox 2/1 fords a stream near Phu Bai
in search of the Vietcong during Operation New York.

Civilian correspondents await a chopper flight back
to Da Nang after a day of covering the war.

A Vietnamese priest accompanies a wounded Vietcong
as he turns himself in for treatment.

Suffer the children who are innocently caught up in the fighting.

A Vietnamese of the right age to be a Vietcong soldier
is brought to the field headquarters as a VC suspect.

The author in his "office" during Operation New York.

Marine of Kilo 3/1 blends in
with his surroundings as he
maneuvers along a hedgerow.

Marine cautiously moves
over an enemy underground
bunker complex.

The Air Was Ours

We controlled the air in South Vietnam, but that doesn't mean the control was limitless. We regularly had planes and helicopters shot out of the air by the enemy. In fact, the Marine Corps lost four hundred sixty-three aircraft in combat, including one hundred ninety-three fixed-wing and two hundred seventy helicopters. The greatest number of fixed wing lost ninety-five F-4 Phantoms. One hundred and nine CH-46 Sea Knight helicopters were lost along with sixty-nine Hueys. I flew in all three gathering stories for *Leatherneck* Magazine.

A Marine Corps F-4 Phantom from the VMFA 323 "Death Rattlers."

Marine mechanics repair the wing tips of an A6 Intruder.

A UH-34D helicopter is guided to its "parking" spot at Tam Ky at the start of Operation Double Eagle II, February 1966.

A CH-46 Sea Knight helicopter approaches a
landing loaded with Marines.

My usual spot beside the door while flying in the UH-34D.

An F-4 Phantom approaches Minh Tan (2) with its payload of 500-pound bombs while Marines of Fox 2/26 attack on the ground through a rice paddy during Operation Independence.

Seven enemy soldiers, captured south of Da Nang, await their transportation off the battlefield onboard a UH-34D helicopter.

Marines of Fox 2/26 conduct a strategic withdrawal with their wounded from the hamlet of Minh Tan (2) after being caught in an ambush during Operation Independence, February 6, 1967.

Marines approach a landing zone while a UH-34D
chopper circles overhead waiting to extract
them from the battlefield.

A damaged UH-1E Huey is "medevaced" for salvage.

Home Sweet Home

Housing in Vietnam was what you made it to be. At division, regiment, or battalion headquarters Marines normally lived in hard tents or sandbagged bunkers. But, in the field it was catch as catch can. The most popular and expedient was the poncho hooch. If you were lucky, you'd find overhead cover, such as a bridge, or vacated plantation home. The idea was to provide cover from the rain, a haven away from the constant buzz of the mosquitoes, and a place to catch a few winks.

Side-by-side low rent quarters for Echo 2/9 Marines in their vacated plantation platoon headquarters ten miles south of Da Nang.

These Marines found a collapsed bridge to set up
their temporary home in the field.

An American flag sent by "Mom"
is prominently displayed at this
Marine's bunker home near First
Marine Division headquarters.

During a torrential rain, occupants
of the bunker simply reached their
canteen cup out the firing hole
to catch "cool, clear" water.

A two-man poncho hooch provide basic protection during monsoon rains.

The five arty FO and radar operator Marines atop Marble Mountain, who kept watch over Da Nang and surrounding area, lived in a corrugated steel hooch.

Not much protection from the rain, but this bombed out plantation building provided a semblance of home for this 2/7 Marine on a sweep of his company's tactical area of operation.

These Marines used grass to make their home in the field.

Wash day in the field.

Salvaged corrugated steel made a good cover
for this "home away from home."

South Vietnamese People

During the Vietnam War, the population of South Vietnam was approximately fifteen million. American forces who served there added another three million, four hundred thousand during the war years of 1961–1975. The Americans and their Allies were sent to that Southeast Asian country to guard against the invading North Vietnamese Army and to protect the people of South Vietnam—young and old alike. Those shown here lived under our protective umbrella in and around Da Nang. When the allies left after the peace treaty of 1973 and the fall of Saigon in 1975, some of these same people left their homeland and came to the United States to begin their life anew. They are now doctors, lawyers, stage and movie stars, authors, business leaders, educators, astronauts, military officers, inventors, and legislators. Today, more than one million, three hundred thousand Vietnamese are living in the United States—three percent of the overall immigrant population of the country. Seventy-six percent of them are now American citizens. The rest have Green Cards.

Cheroot-smoking Vietnamese farmer.

A survivor of the French-Indochina
and Vietnam War.

Coconut harvest

Basket weaver takes his product to market.

By the time the war ended, these boys
probably were carrying real guns.

Black market vendor with her wares in Da Nang.

Balancing mamasan's load.

Diarrhea claimed this mother's child.

Young boy takes charge
of his water buffalo

Vietnamese USO troupe from Saigon
entertains Marines at Da Nang.

Precarious escape from the blistering sun.

Young Vietnamese girl in her ao dai.

Must be fish Friday

The Enemy

The American fighting men in Vietnam faced a variety of enemies: the terrain, the weather, antiwar demonstrators back home, elected officials on Capitol Hill, but primarily the North Vietnamese or NVA or PAVN mainline soldiers and the Vietcong guerrillas. When not actively searching for the enemy or dropping leaflets asking them to surrender, we were constantly on the lookout for their booby traps. Allied forces lost more than two hundred eighty-two men and women in Vietnam. More than four hundred forty-four enemy were killed along with six hundred twenty-seven civilians in both North and South Vietnam.

A pair of Vietcong suspects are brought in for questioning.

Captured North Vietnamese soldiers during
Operation Independence, February 1967.

A wounded Vietcong received
medical treatment.

Captured NVA soldier awaits
transportation from the battlefield.

Wounded NVA soldier is treated
at the medical center in An Hoa.

Captured Vietcong guerrilla soldier
is questioned in the field.

Forlorn Vietcong captured
south of Da Nang.

Interpreter fills out the capture tag
for another Vietcong.

Lieutenant General Lewis Walt and Glenn Ford

Actor Glenn Ford spent a month in Vietnam in 1967 searching for talent for a future film about Marines. Ford had served as an enlisted Marine in World War II. In 1958, he was commissioned in the Navy. When I caught up with him in Vietnam, he was a Navy reserve lieutenant commander public affairs officer. He retired in 1979 as a captain. I spent two days with him in February 1967 when he was a guest of Lieutenant General Lewis Walt, commanding general of the Third Marine Amphibious Force and commander of all of I Corps. I was gathering material for a story on LtGen Walt at the time for *Leatherneck* Magazine.

LtGen Lewis Walt and Glenn Ford enjoy a chat with
Marines preparing a new defensive position
on the perimeter of Camp Carroll.

Ford is introduced to a Marine fan.

Ford sees the results of war up close and personal.
A pair of KIA South Vietnamese soldiers
leave the field in a jeep.

Ford autographs a 175mm artillery round
before it is fired at an enemy target
in northern I Corps.

LtGen Walt briefs Ford as they
hop from one base to another
in his command chopper.

An after-dinner cigar caps a field meal and a long
day of visiting bases in northern I Corps.

Snap Shots

Photographers make photos that record the history of our times. They also make photos of their friends, events that interest them, their family, and other things and people that catch their eye. Here are a few of my "snap shot" memories.

A Marine on patrol in Vietnam, captured in a nature's frame of fallen banana trees.

"You got some candy, mister?"

Larry Czonka, future NFL Hall of Fame running back for the Miami Dolphins, watches the Syracuse defense perform during his final year of college ball, 1967.

A Syracuse student tells his girlfriend he has received his draft notice and will soon report for boot camp and eventual duty in Vietnam.

The author and lifelong buddy, Claude "Sonny" Bice
celebrate the Marine Corps birthday, November 10, 1979,
at American Legion Post 364, Woodbridge, Virginia.

The Smartsy twins, Marine Sergeants Dean and Dennis,
liked to play chess when not on a long-range patrol
or cooking a meal for men of the 1st Marine
Recon Battalion on Hill 327, 1968.

Experimental ears designed to hear the enemy at great distances. Problem was the ears would also pick up everything between the Marine with the ears and his objective across the rice paddy. Mice sounded like elephants tramping through the weeds.

Believe it or not, that's a Marine in the making.

Good things my knees were cropped out.

Uncle Sam and Lady Liberty accompany the
children at the Dale City July 4th Parade, 1993.

Available transportation in Vietnam.

Cooking burgers for the patients at the McGuire VA Hospital in Richmond, VA, with Post 364 Commander Marty Rhyne looking on.

Beware when you make a membership bet with the Ladies Auxiliary in Virginia. You may lose and have to pay the piper.

EPILOGUE

My wife, Helen, began losing weight in 2009. The following year, I was elected President of the Virginia Society of the Sons of the American Revolution. And I began gathering material for this book.

Helen accompanied me on all of my travels in Virginia and throughout the United States. We visited at least a dozen different specialists in Northern Virginia that year in search of a cause for her weight loss. No luck. A visit to the head of the gastroenterology department at Georgetown University, Washington, D.C., produced no results. Three visits to the Mayo Clinic in Jacksonville, Florida, were a waste of time, as were three trips to the University of Virginia Medical Center in Charlottesville.

Shortly after being elected Historian General of the National Society of the SAR in July 2012, it became apparent to me that I would not be able to fulfill my one-year term. Helen could no longer travel with me and I decided that calls home to check on her while I was on the road were not adequate. I needed to be with her each day. So, a few days before Christmas that year, I notified President General Steve Leishman that I would resign, effective January 1. He understood and was fully supportive.

Helen was upset with my decision. She did not want to be the cause of me giving up something I had worked so hard to achieve. I told her that's what husbands are for. Case closed.

Health issues soon began visiting my doorstep—gout in my right ankle, eczema, continuing degeneration of a COPD condition, sleep apnea, and stress fractures of three toes. On one routine visit to my primary care physician, Dr. Bozena Wolanska, she said, "Bob, you're a basket case." I had cut back on my SAR activities to monitor Helen's health, but had overlooked taking care of myself.

To make good use of my time in bed, I culled through all of my old photographs looking for oldies that documented my life, and those I had made in Vietnam during my career as a Marine Corps combat correspondent. I digitized all of the photos I had negatives for by scanning and uploading them to my computer.

When the summer of 2013 arrived, Helen had reached a point where she had stopped losing weight—wasn't gaining much, but wasn't losing any either. But, she was diagnosed with Alzheimer's, a debilitating disease that affects the memory.

My health had taken a turn for the better and Helen was getting a little tired of my cooking. She encouraged me to get back on the SAR campaign trail, which I did, announcing my candidacy for Registrar General. When the closing date of the candidacy period arrived, I was the only announced candidate for that office. I had driven more than 10,000 miles presenting my credentials, and received the endorsement of every state and district I visited. That was to be short lived. In December 2013, my wife took another turn for the worse and once again I was forced to cancel my campaign for high office. Back to the book.

Having been born in 1941, I am officially a member of the Silent Generation (1925–1941), but my friends continuously urged me to write this book. I could be silent no more.

This has not been an easy write. I'm a bonafide pack rat. I have squirreled away memorabilia all my life. This was both a Godsend and a curse when it came time to gather material for my book. What should I include? What should set aside? In the final analysis, it's better to have more than not enough.

If you've read everything that preceded this epilogue, you now have a fairly good handle on the life I've led these past seventy-six years.

My first wife and I parted ways in 1979. I remarried in 1982. Helen, my "now" wife of thirty-four years, had three children by a previous marriage, Brenda, Michael, and Brian. Between them and my children—Jack, Donna, Bob, Alan, and Brian, Helen and I have eight grown children, twenty grandchildren, and twenty-one great-grandchildren.

As this book was undergoing its final edit, I was contacted by the Freedom Museum in Manassas, Virginia, and asked if I would be interested in preparing some of my Vietnam photos for presentation on three four by eight foot panels on a continuing basis. I agreed and during the first five months of the program's existence, I prepared displays on scout dogs, the enemy, enlisted combat Marines, crew-served weapons, the South Vietnamese people, and the first 140mm rocket attack on Da Nang. Ten or more additional displays were being planned. One of the museum sponsors, a local Chick-fil-A restaurant, displayed a selection of my combat photos on a single four by eight foot panel in Bristow, Virginia.

Bob Gassaway, the former AP war correspondent who wrote the foreword to this memoir, regrettably passed away in May 2016 and never got to see the final product. We had exchanged email two months prior when I gave him an update on the progress being made on the book. He was supportive to the end.

When I finished this memoir, I had served twenty years in the Marine Corps, including some twenty months as a combat correspondent in Vietnam, fourteen years with the Voice of America, two years with the State Department and Justice Department, more than fifty years a member of the American Legion, and sixteen years as a member of the National Society, Sons of the American Revolution. It's time to take off my pack.

And, on that note, I'll sign off by saying "sine die."

ABOUT THE AUTHOR

Captain Robert L. "Bob" Bowen, USMC, Retired

Captain Robert L. "Bob" Bowen was born January 12, 1941. He enlisted in the Marine Corps in 1960 and served tours at Quantico, the Armed Forces Radio and Television Station on Okinawa, and *Leatherneck* Magazine. While at *Leatherneck*, Bob served three tours as a combat correspondent in Vietnam. He was selected to attend a special graduate-level, two-semester program (1967–1968) in photojournalism at Syracuse University, Syracuse, New York, where he graduated first in his class. His reward was another tour as a combat correspondent in Vietnam, this time with the First Marine Division. Bob was selected for warrant officer in 1969 and promoted in 1970. While serving as Chief, Photojournalism Instructor at the Defense Information School in Indianapolis, Indiana, he was selected for the Limited Duty Officer program and promoted a first lieutenant. A four-year tour as Station Manager of the Far East Radio and Television Station at Misawa Air Base, Japan, followed. Captain Bowen retired in 1980, while serving as the Marine Corps Spokesman in the Office of the Assistant Secretary of Defense for Public Affairs at the Pentagon.

Bob retired a second time in 1996 following government service as a public affairs officer and writer editor with the State Department, Justice Department, and Voice of America.

Military medals and decorations include Bronze Star with Combat V, Purple Heart Medal, Defense Meritorious Service Medal, Air Force Meritorious Service Medal, Navy Commendation Medal with Combat

V, Navy Achievement Medal with Bronze Star in lieu of second award, and Combat Action Ribbon, among others.

Photos made by Captain Bob Bowen in Vietnam earned him the title "Runner-up, Military Photographer of the Year" in 1967. He was inducted into Kappa Alpha Mu, the National Honorary Fraternity in Photojournalism at the University of Missouri, Columbia, in 1972.

While still serving on active duty, Bob served as Commander of Woodbridge Post 364 of the American Legion. He served as Virginia's State Commander of the Legion in 1991–1992 and as National Vice Commander in 1996–1997.

Bob is also active in the National Society of the Sons of the American Revolution. He has served as President of the Fielding Lewis Chapter in Fredericksburg, Virginia, President of the Virginia Society of the SAR in 2010–2011, National Vice President General in 2007–2008, and Historian General in 2013–2014.

Bob and Helen, his wife of thirty-four years, have made their retirement home in Fredericksburg, Virginia.

Robin Kern

Robin Kern worked twenty-four years as graphic specialist and editor for the Department of Defense at Fort Leavenworth, Kansas. She is currently a DoD contractor providing graphic and archival support at Fort Leavenworth.

Robin created graphics for several commercially published books including *Abandoning Vietnam: How America Left and South Vietnam Lost Its War* (James H. Willbanks, 2004), *The Tet Offensive: A Concise History* (Willbanks, 2005), *Army Raiders: The Special Activities Group in Korea* (Rich Kiper, 2010), and *A Raid Too Far: Operation Lam Son 719 and Vietnamization in Laos* (Willbanks, 2014). She was editor on the soon to be published book, *Duty First: 1ˢᵗ Infantry Division Cold War to Victory in Operation Desert Storm* (Greg Fontenot, 2017).

Printed in the United States
By Bookmasters

Printed in the United States
By Bookmasters